EVENING STREET REVIEW

NUMBER 26, MID-AUTUMN 2020

*Hi Bridget,
Here's wishing you a safe,
virus-free, Happy Thanksgiving!
luv ya,
J. P. Daley*

. . .all men and women are created equal in rights to life, liberty, and the pursuit of happiness.

—Elizabeth Cady Stanton, revision of the
American Declaration of Independence, 1848

PUBLISHED TWICE (OR MORE) A YEAR
BY
EVENING STREET PRESS

Editor & Managing Editor: Barbara Bergmann
Associate Editors: Donna Spector, Kailen Nourse-Driscoll, Patti Sullivan, Anthony Mohr, L D Zane, Stacia Levy, Jeffrey Davis, Dana Stamps II, Clela Reed, Matthew Mendoza

Founding Editor: Gordon Grigsby

Evening Street Review is published in the spring and fall of every year (with additional issues as needed) by Evening Street Press. United States subscription rates are $24 for two issues and $44 for four issues (individuals), and $32 for two issues and $52 for four issues (institutions).

Back cover art by Patti Sullivan

Library of Congress Control Number: 2020940685

ISBN: 978-1-937347-60-4

Evening Street Review is centered on the belief that all men and women are created equal, that they have a natural claim to certain inalienable rights, and that among these are the rights to life, liberty, and the pursuit of happiness. With this center, and an emphasis on writing that has both clarity and depth, it practices the widest eclecticism. Evening Street Review reads submissions of poetry (free verse, formal verse, and prose poetry) and prose (short stories and creative nonfiction) year round. Submit 3-6 poems or 1-2 prose pieces at a time. Payment is one contributor's copy. Copyright reverts to author upon publication. Response time is 3-6 months. Please address submissions to Editors, 2881 Wright St, Sacramento, CA 95821-4819. Email submissions are also acceptable; send to the following address as Microsoft Word or rich text files (.rtf): **editor@eveningstreetpress.com**.

For submission guidelines, subscription information, published works, and author profiles, please visit our website:
www.eveningstreetpress.com.

EVENING STREET REVIEW
PUBLISHED BY EVENING STREET PRESS

NUMBER 26, MID-AUTUMN 2020

CONTENTS

POETRY (cont)

FICTION

NONFICTION

OCCASIONAL NOTES:
WE STILL NEED HEROES

In early May 2020 a prisoner sent us a poem:

TONY VICK
WE STILL NEED HEROES

Sometimes we get lost in the
hateful rhetoric presented to
us—perhaps out of fear or
uncomfortable confrontation

The idea that racism is a
disease that has been eradicated
is only a notion believed by
people who are not on the
receiving end of the stinging
words of old Jim Crow

So -

We still need heroes

MLK and Rosa Parks are
in the history books—but history
continues to be made—lived—
suffered

So -

We still need heroes

Cleverly disguising words of hate
and dehumanizing people through
the safety of the world wide web
has invigorated the masses into
a new form of racism
The kind that may not be
politically correct to speak

but is still tolerated in unspoken
actions and in laws and policies
and undermining events every day

So -

We still need heroes

We need the strength and
courage of a few to embolden
us to action, to speech, to change.
We are a part of this time of
history, the part we are
accountable for.

So -

We still need heroes.

Will you be one?

Vick

On the 25th, George Floyd was murdered by a police officer. Millions of people around the world stood up and cried, "Say their names." There are so many. And many being added all too often.

What will you do?

When you see one of "them" will you think about their safety and not yours (especially in segregated neighborhoods)? If you talk to people on the street, will you salute everyone (not especially "them" because it's the right thing to do)? Will you call out racist language in yourself and others? When you try to do something for one of "them," will you do it because they are human, therefore one of "us"? Will you support reparations for Blacks (back pay for slaves, 40 acres and a mule) and Indigenous populations (payment for stolen lands)?

"We still need heroes. / Will you be one?"

BB

TONY VICK
REMEMBERING

I visit every day at lunch time
  bringing with me your favorite things:
       Biscuits from Loveless Cafe
       Chicken and dumplings from Cracker Barrel
       or those coconut covered marshmallows from Walmart

Surrounded by those things you love:
       Our wedding day picture, in that silver frame your
        Aunt Mable gave you on our 25th anniversary.
       A picture of David when you first tried to swaddle him.
       The quilt you made from all your old dresses and my shirts.
       The hairbrush your mama gave you on your 18th birthday.
I brush your hair and sing some of the songs we love:
       Ring of Fire
       Amazing Grace
       Evergreen
I wait for you to tell me to shut up that I can't sing.
I look for a toe tap or your mouth to move at the chorus.
Nothing.

I watch you eat
  waiting for an expression of remembrance.
Nothing.
No hint that you have any special affection
  for the food or me.

           ...Now I see you on Thursdays.
You rock by the window in that old wooden chair,
  the same one you rocked our baby boy in.
If he had lived past his twenty-second birthday
  he would have been sixty today.
You eat bland vegetables and cut up boiled chicken.
Your arms are moving fork to mouth—just muscle
  memory programmed to eat, with no feeling or expression.

(cont)

Your eyes avoid my eyes like our puppy did
  when you caught him shredding up the
  morning newspaper.
They're still as blue as the ocean
  with little specks of silver.

You've left me and yet you are still here.
Your body is warm, your heart beating, I want
  to snuggle up against you and just sleep — it would
  seem adulterous since you have vacated your body.
You slipped away so gradually that I was not prepared.
When do I pack up your things and let you go?

Pastor Knight asked me on March 25, 1956 if I
  would keep you in sickness and in health,
  for better or for worse.

I call on Sundays now and Nurse Karen
  puts the phone by your ear so I can tell
  you I love you.
I don't drive anymore, my eyes don't allow it.
The church brings me a plate lunch each day.
I eat at noon, so we can eat together in spirit.

I've got all my favorite things around me:
        The baseball glove I gave David when he was six.
        The handkerchief you put in my pocket every
          moming when I was leaving for work that
          smelled of your perfume.
        The picture of the three of us on David's
          graduation day.

I eat the food the church brings it doesn't
  taste like your cooking.
The old record is playing and I listen to
  Johnny and June.
I sing along and tell myself
        "I still can't sing."

But you already knew that.   *Vick*

DENNIS VANNATTA
BLACK AND WHITE AND A CERTAIN SHADE OF GREEN:
MY LIFE IN LIVING COLOR

A box unopened for decades can be a treasure chest, but beware it wasn't previously owned by Pandora.

I was recently going through a box filled with a little of this and that—old documents, photos, a baby's bonnet, etc.—that had belonged to my late mother. Among them was a letter my father wrote her in the summer of 1948 when he was working on his Master of Education degree at The University of Missouri in Columbia. She had stayed home to tend us kids in Appleton City, where my father was superintendent of schools. In the letter he asked my mother to make sure Bill mowed the grass at "the colored school."

The "colored" shocked me. My father was a gentle man, humane and sensitive. He was also a Roosevelt liberal. I couldn't believe he'd have even a smidgen of racial bigotry. But then I reflected, no, "colored" and "Negro" would not have carried connotations of bigotry then, seven decades ago. By the mid-1960s, though, the cultural climate had changed, and even the well-meaning older labels were frowned upon by "Black people," the preferred new label and the one I, a child of the '60s, still instinctively use. In its turn, "Black" gave way to "African American." Today, unless I'm behind the times (altogether possible), "person of color" is preferred.

But back to "the colored school." If it was "colored" that first struck me, "school" is what I still haven't quite gotten over. There was a colored *school* in Appleton City? I didn't even remember Black *people* in Appleton City.

Appleton City was a tiny hamlet, 1,050 souls in the 1950 census. We moved to the big city of Sedalia in 1954 when I was not quite eight, and I remember pointing out the injustice of being uprooted from familiar surroundings by claiming that I knew each of the thousand-odd inhabitants by name. Obviously, that was absurd, but the fact that I thought I did makes it all the more puzzling—baffling—that apparently among those I could name was not one Black person. Today I can vividly recall many details about Appleton City—the smell of the depot agent's pipe tobacco, the shifting colors of the juke box in the Blue Inn café, the cuspidors glimpsed in the beer joint on Main when the front door was thrown open—but I cannot recall a single Black person living in the town of my birth.

I phoned my sister, seven years my senior. She confirmed it: "Of course there were Black people. Don't you remember they had to use the back door of our store? They weren't allowed to use the front doors of White stores." For one year before we moved to Sedalia, my parents owned a little grocery. I remember a poor old White woman named Frony who would steal pop bottles from the back of our store and bring them around to the front and resell them. I thought she was a witch, and even today just thinking the name "Frony" gives me the shivers. But I don't recall Black people entering our store through any door.

Didn't I remember, my sister asked, when my parents bought the first new car they'd ever owned, a two-tone green and white Pontiac, and the very first day they drove it downtown and parked it on Main Street, the preacher at the Black church ran into it? No, I did not.

So there'd been a Black church, too. Where was it? She couldn't remember. Where was the Black school? She couldn't remember. Where had the Black people lived? (They would have had their own section of town, of course.) She couldn't remember. Yes, my sister was one-up on me, but she didn't have a lot to brag about. Why did we between us remember so little?

Unless the Black people just really didn't count.

*

We moved to Sedalia, population of around 25,000, in 1954. It was there that my memory of living in the same community as Black people begins.

There is a statue of a generic World War I Doughboy on the courthouse lawn, but the only memorial to an actual individual that I'm aware of in Sedalia is to a Black man, Scott Joplin, King of Ragtime, who wrote his famous "Maple Leaf Rag" in Sedalia. The memorial is in a parking lot where the Maple Leaf Tavern once stood on Main Street. Sedalia even has a Scott Joplin festival in the summer.

Neither the memorial nor festival existed until after I was grown and had moved away. Certainly, no Black man was ever honored in Sedalia in my lifetime. Probably the most famous Black man was the owner of the whorehouse in the shadow of the viaduct north of Main. In my time no Black man was seen south of Main except on rare occasions when he had a very good reason for being there, and he'd better be able to explain that reason to the White cop who was sure to stop him and demand to know what he was doing on the White side of town.

We called north of Main, where the Blacks lived, Niggertown.

I knew little more about their lives there than I knew about Black people in Appleton City, which was nothing. I'm sure they had their own church, probably more than one, but I don't remember them. No doubt they had their own stores because they didn't use ours, but where were they? Dunno. Did they have their own hospital? When I was ten, I spent two weeks battling rheumatic fever in Bothwell Hospital in Sedalia; I never saw a Black patient there, much less a Black nurse or doctor.

I do remember the Black school, Hubbard. My grade school, mighty Mark Twain, lost only one game in any sport all year, in basketball to Hubbard grade school, whose players sported mustaches, could slap the backboard, and were beaten with a belt by their coach for misplays. We were so entertained by the spectacle that we didn't even mind losing, and when we get together at high school reunions we will still laugh to think about it. (Well, truthfully, I never actually saw those mustaches, slapped backboards, and beatings because I didn't play basketball, but I still laugh right along with the others.)

Sedalia schools were integrated in the early 1960s when I was in high school. Sort of. As I understood it at the time, a Black student could attend a White school if his parents requested it. Perhaps there was more to it than that, but all I know for a fact is that we had approximately a dozen Black students in my senior class of nearly three-hundred at Smith-Cotton, the previously all-White high school.

The vast majority of Black students still attended Hubbard High. They had their own prom. (My God, attend *our* prom? Be serious.) The Hubbard prom queen's picture appeared in our *Archives*, the Smith-Cotton High yearbook, along with four photos of White "queens" reigning over various dances, one not being enough for us, obviously. In the "Tiger Tails" section, there are twenty-four pages of White students involved in various activities, two for Blacks.

Oh. We were egalitarian in one regard. We allowed, no doubt encouraged, Black students to play on Smith-Cotton's sports teams. Indeed, if they wanted to play sports, they had no choice but to play for "us." Hubbard High no longer had sports teams. Why would they need teams? We were integrated, after all.

To the best of my recollection, the first words I ever exchanged with a Black person were at a high school basketball game my senior year. After a titanic struggle, Smith-Cotton defeated mighty Columbia Hickman, a rare accomplishment, thanks in part to "our" six-foot-nine giant, Richard Cole, who happened to be Black. As I exited the gym alongside other joyous fans, I happened to glance at a young Black man. "Helluva game," he said. I agreed: "Helluva game." Fifty-three years later, I still remember that historic event: I'd actually exchanged words with a Black person!

*

You'd think I would have had more involvement with Black people when I went away to college at Central Missouri State, to which students came not just from the hinterlands of the state but Kansas City, St. Louis, and beyond.

I had no Black professors at Central Missouri. Perhaps I had Black students in class with me, but I don't recall a single one. We had Black players on the basketball team, of course. The Fighting Mules were pretty good, thanks largely to Cozell Walker and Calvin Petit. "Throw that ball to Calvin! Let Calvin shoot that ball!" Blacks in the stands would holler, and we Whites would laugh to hear them. They were a caution!

The one scene involving race that I recall from my college days, although even here no Black person makes an appearance, occurred after the assassination of Martin Luther King and the subsequent riots in cities across America. A knot of White students were gathered in the lobby of the student union, studying something that one of them held. I went over for a look. It was a map of Kansas City. "They can take this block. And they can take this block. They can burn the shit out of everything all the way to this street if they want to. But if they try to cross *this* street, that's when we'll blow their Black asses away."

Yes, America was a war zone in 1968, but the battles were fought almost entirely in Black neighborhoods with almost entirely Black casualties. I'd shake my head to see the news reports on TV, but as long as they stayed on the other side of *that street*, I wasn't too bothered.

*

I suddenly found it impossible to keep a safe distance when in June 1969 I was drafted into Uncle Sam's Army. A group of us reluctant warriors (all White as I recall), gathered at the depot on the north side of the tracks in Sedalia and then rode the train to the induction center in Kansas City. After the customary pleasantries there, we took the bus to Ft. Leonard Wood, arrived well after dark, and were deposited onto a parking lot beside a dismal wooden barracks, where we stood waiting for someone to take us in hand.

Something struck the pavement near me. Then another one. Rocks! Rocks were falling out of the night sky all around us. From the other side of the barracks came a voice shouting for order, threats of dire consequences if any more rocks were thrown. Then from around the barracks came a White sergeant, who jerked his thumb in the direction the rocks had come from and said with the closest thing to sympathy I heard from anyone of that rank for a good long while, "A bus load of niggers from Chicago."

Four weeks later, Apollo 11 circled the moon, and to celebrate the occasion we were given three-day passes, probably the first and last basic trainees so blessed. We could take advantage of the opportunity, however, only if we could prove we could get to our homes and back to Ft. Lost in the Woods in those three days. That is, we had to live in fairly close driving distance, as all of us Sedalians did, or had to show our drill sergeant a purchased round-trip airline or bus ticket. A baby-faced Black recruit sat on his bunk across from me, eyes welling with tears. He didn't have the fifty dollars for a bus ticket to Chicago. I don't recall mulling it over much. I just reached into my wallet, took out two twenties and a ten, and handed them to him. My friends (White) were incredulous. "You dumb son of a bitch, you'll never see him or that money again!" "Oh well," I said. Seventy-two hours later, the baby-faced Black guy was back, and the first thing he did was hand me the fifty dollars.

What had happened in the four weeks between my ducking rocks thrown by "niggers from Chicago" and my handing one of them fifty dollars? I'd slept beside Black men in barracks, showered and shaved beside them, marched with them, fired M-14s beside them, cussed sergeants Black and White (behind their backs, of course) right along with them. I'd actually met Black people, lived with them, found they were just folks, just like us Whites, all a part of the same humanity, the world full of rainbows for those who have eyes to see.

Well . . .

The Black recruit I loaned the money to? We were polite to one another, but despite living for eight weeks in the same seven-man room we never shared a single conversation. Nor did I with any of the other Black soldiers in my platoon. Predictable with ol' rural Missouri redneck me involved, you say? I plead not guilty—or at least no more guilty than anyone else. In a world (the military) where close friendships were forged almost instantly, I did not know of a single friendship between Black and White. Polite, maybe even cordial, yes; friendship, no.

I can extend this to my entire Army experience: no friendships that I can recall between Black and White. And that cordiality that one occasionally saw was most often only a brittle veneer threatening to crack and reveal something ugly, even dangerous, underneath.

My kumbaya memory of loaning fifty dollars to the Black guy was more than counterbalanced by two other recollections of Black/White relations in basic training. The first I didn't witness but only heard about. It involved my best friend in basic, Gary, of Pittsburg, Kansas, who looked like he was chiseled out of a boulder with a head shaped like and about the size of an upside-down peck basket. It happened in the PX where we recruits were allowed to go buy supplies and drink beer (which was encouraged, beer drinkers being fightin' men) every couple of weeks. Gary had had a beer or three and was on the patio enjoying the country songs he'd paid for on the juke box when some Black soldiers came out, unplugged the juke box (thereby canceling Gary's songs), plugged it back in, and punched in some soul songs. Gary offered a polite objection. He was surrounded by Blacks. The next instant Blacks were seen flying in every direction trying to escape Hurricane Gary. Oh, didn't we (Whites) laugh to tell it, laugh to hear it. What would our reaction have been if the races had been reversed? You know.

The other anecdote this time involved me. It was the last day of basic training. We'd all received our orders for various Advanced Individual Training schools, but before we could leave we had to sign out of the company in a very precise fashion using a rather complex form, especially troublesome if one happened to be drunk at the time, as most of us were. One soldier per platoon was assigned to take the form around and see to it that everyone filled it out correctly. In my platoon, the lucky devil was smart-ass, four-eyed college-boy Vannatta. There were a number of college grads but also others who were semi-literate at best. One of the latter category was a tiny Black recruit. Even sober he'd have had trouble doing more than signing his name; drunk, he couldn't fill out a single line or even give me the information to fill it in for him. I pleaded, cajoled, threatened. Somehow I got it done, by which point the guy was, I kid you not, crying. This did not go over well with his best friend, who just happened to be the biggest, baddest Black guy in the platoon. He came to my room, enraged. I can still see him filling the entire doorway, calling my name, calling me out. I was terrified. It was Gary who went out, though, took the Black giant by the arm and led him away. I don't know what transpired between them, but I was saved, and grateful to my White savior.

From basic I went to MP school and then West Point, where we MPs were glorified campus cops. Beautiful setting. Lots of time off. Free bus rides into New York City, free tickets to Broadway plays. Many Black soldiers among the MPs, our sergeants or officers? Nope. Draw your own conclusions.

After six months at West Point I was shipped to Germany where we MPs were tower rats guarding nuclear weapons bunkers. There were Black MPs there; I was friendly with some but friends with none. I recall no friendships between White and Black.

One day I was in the almost deserted barracks when I happened upon a couple of Black guys deep in conversation. When they realized someone else was in the barracks, they hushed up, but then saw it was me and said, "Oh, it's Vannatta. Hey, come on over to HQ with us."

By HQ they meant the smaller barracks housing headquarters company, almost entirely Black (except for officers, of course). A dozen or so Black soldiers were gathered there, looking not at all happy to see a honky coming in. "It's OK, it's Vannatta, he's OK," one of my new Black "friends" said. Then they all resumed their conversation about just how much more shit they were going to take from whitey (not much) and what they were going to do once they stopped taking it. It wasn't going to be nice. I was scared, frankly, shitless and was ready to weep in relief when after a couple of minutes they let me make some lame excuse and leave.

What were they so mad about? That's what we Whites wanted to know. It seemed to us that Black soldiers got every break in the book. Cushier jobs. Fewer work details. Faster promotions. They didn't have to keep their hair cut as short as we did. I got called up before the first sergeant because my mustache wasn't trimmed quite neatly enough. A number of Black soldiers, claiming sensitive skin, were allowed to grow beards. So what the hell did they have to complain about?

One day we got a new Black platoon sergeant. He called us together for a little talk to introduce himself and his expectations. He wasn't out to ride us, make our lives hard. For him it was live and let live as long as we did our jobs. One thing, though: we were never, ever to call him a nigger. I can still see him walking across the parking lot away from our barracks when Bobby from Michigan hollered down from a second-floor window, "You mother fucking nigger!" Sarge paused just an instant, then his shoulders sagged, and he walked on.

*

After the Army, I went to grad school and got my PhD in 1978, a year in which *The Chronicle of Higher Education,* I believe it was, reported that there were two-hundred applicants for each tenure-track job opening in English. I sent out dozens of applications and got one request for an interview, at the University of Arkansas at Little Rock. I could have wept in gratitude at the chance at a tenure-track job. My wife, from Queens, New York, wasn't quite so sanguine. What, live in the *South*? Yes, there was that issue.

Since there's absolutely no point to this memoir if I'm not going to be honest, I have to admit that my biggest fear was that this urban university in a Southern city would be predominantly Black. I was pleasantly surprised—again, being honest here—to find that UALR was only around fifteen percent Black. Jumping ahead three-and-a-half decades, by the time I retired the percentage of Black students had grown to between thirty and forty percent. By then I'd discovered that the color of the student made no difference in my teaching experience. I enjoyed interacting with students (except in 8:00 a.m. classes), and the likeable Black students were just as pleasant as the likeable White ones while the irritating Black students were just as big a pain in the ass as the irritating White ones, but no more so. In fact, over the course of my career I had no major problems and few minor with any students, Black or White.

Let's back down off that rainbow bridge for a moment, though. I have a feeling I was more satisfied by my experience at UALR than many Black students were. They came hoping that a university education would be the route to a better life—and then most of them disappeared. The percentage of Black students plummeted between lower- and upper-level courses. What happened to them? I'm not claiming racial prejudice was involved. From what I could tell, administrators did their best, and still are doing their best, to help Black students. But it's a tough battle. Maybe it was already lost for many of them before they set foot on campus.

What did I do to help? Nothing. Except . . .

I blush to admit it, but the truth is I had a hard time not giving Black students "the benefit of the doubt" when grading. Much as I fought against it, I'd wind up convincing myself that a no more than competently written essay by a Black student was really quite good and a pretty good one truly excellent. Was that prejudice? Yes, indeed.

I can't recall seeing examples of active prejudice at UALR from others. There was the story, though, related by a young Black assistant professor who had gone to UALR as an undergraduate. When she told her adviser back then, a grand old Southern gentleman right out of Hollywood casting, that she wanted to go to graduate school and be a professor, he eyed her sympathetically and skeptically and purred, "Perhaps you should consider domestic work." He was still on the faculty when she returned to UALR to teach.

*

I worked at the university; I didn't live there. What was the Little Rock that we moved to in 1978 like, in racial terms? This was the city, remember, to which a scant twenty years before Ike sent the troops to enforce integration at Central High.[*]

---

[*] An aside. Most Arkansans—and Americans in general, I assume—think of the Central High integration crisis as a stain on the honor of the city and state. This, I

By 1978, the schools had been integrated, stores and restaurants were prohibited by law from refusing service on the basis of race, in some neighborhoods Blacks lived side by side with Whites, and Arkansas had just elected Bill Clinton, "the boy governor," surely one of the most liberal in the South if not nation.

But look more closely—damn those closer looks!—and you find that, yes, schools were integrated, but what this meant in practice was that Whites by the thousand were fleeing to Conway, Cabot, Bryant, and other nearby cities, and many of those who stayed, and could afford to, sent their children to Catholic School for Boys, Mount St. Mary Academy, and Pulaski Academy, leaving the public schools mostly Black. And if Blacks could legally patronize White stores and restaurants, you tended to see them only in certain ones: K-Mart but not M. M. Cohn, McDonald's but not Restaurant Jacques and Suzanne. Those neighborhoods where Blacks lived alongside Whites? They were called "transition neighborhoods," where you did not want to be if you owned your house and were White. As for Bill Clinton, bless his heart, Bill was the Kardashian of politics. He looked good on camera, he was successful (at getting elected), but what exactly did he *do*? Damned if I know.

What about the Vannattas of the '70s and '80s? We were sending our children to Catholic schools. I could claim it was because my wife and children were Catholic, my wife never having set foot in a public school of any kind until graduate school (whereas I, Baptist, had gone only to public schools), but the truth is I did not want my children going to mostly Black schools. Perhaps they would have done well there, been happy and helped make the world, racially, a better place. But I was not going to risk my children in a social experiment.

Until we moved to lily-White west Little Rock in 1985, we lived in a transition neighborhood in southwest Little Rock. We didn't realize it was in transition when we first moved there. I was an untenured assistant professor, my wife had not yet found a job, and the little house in the middle-class neighborhood was all we could afford. We were content with the house and neighborhood—at first. True, there was one Black family a block over, another one down that way, but so what? We weren't

---

believe, is itself racist because it implies that history is White, that all that counts in our judgments are the Whites who snarled and spat and threatened and shouted, "Nigger go home!" But what about those nine courageous Black youths who walked with dignity and resolve through that terrifying gauntlet? How many cities and states can record in their histories such valor and nobility from their young people?

prejudiced. Live and let live. We soon learned, though, that in Southern cities at that time it was pointless to think in terms of a neighborhood with a few Black families. Rather, there were neighborhoods with a few Black families *today*, but tomorrow there would be several more Black families, then several more the next day until there were mostly Black families, and good luck trying to sell your house then.

We stuck it out seven years. Then our next-door neighbors with children almost exactly the same age as ours put their house on the market when the husband got a job in Russellville. Even then we hesitated. It wasn't until they'd moved out and we stared at the empty house with the for sale sign on the front lawn that we took the plunge. We talked to a real estate agent on a Saturday. She'd get the ball rolling, and our house would be on the market with a for sale sign on our lawn within a week. Mid-week next week our sign was not yet up, but the sign next door was down, and a new family was moving in, the wife Asian, the husband Black, their little boy Black with Asian features. The next day—I swear to God, the very next day—there was our for sale sign on our front lawn. We couldn't look our new neighbors in the eye. They didn't bother looking our way.[*]

*

We moved in 1985 to more upscale, White west Little Rock. "I guess I'll have to keep my yard mowed now," I joked to a colleague. "You don't keep your yard mowed out there and they'll burn a cross on your lawn," he said. I laughed.

*

That was three decades ago. Have things changed? I guess. Some. There are more Black people with money now. One wouldn't bat an eye to see a Black person in any store or restaurant in Little Rock. We have a Black city manager and a Black chief of police. That's all good, progress, nothing to sneeze at. Most minimum wage jobs are held by Black people, though. The public schools have only gotten Blacker. The percentage of Black students at UALR has risen, but I seriously doubt that the number of Black professors has risen to match it. And if not so long ago real estate agents would direct Black clients away from White neighborhoods (it was rumored and I'm inclined to believe it) while today Blacks are free to live in any neighborhood they can afford to buy into, the vast majority still live

---

[*] Anecdote. Ten or so years later, my son's mediocre soccer team got a welcome addition: a big, fast, strong Black young man with Asian features. Nice kid. Nice family. Were they the same family who'd moved in to the house next to ours in southwest Little Rock? Sure. Did they know? I wouldn't be at all surprised. I never had the courage to bring it up, explain. But what would I have explained?

east of University and south of Markham where, at night and sometimes in the daytime, it's a war zone. I do not exaggerate. Drive-by shootings, armed robberies, gang violence are daily occurrences. On a recent night twenty-five people were wounded in a shoot-out at a nightclub, all Black. The city's solution? Close the night club. I rather doubt that that gets at the root of the problem. What would I do if I were king? I have no idea. I'm White, after all. What do I know?

*

That lily-White west Little Rock neighborhood we moved into in 1985 is now in transition. Our neighborhood is not even called west Little Rock anymore; now we're "midtown." West Little Rock is now several miles farther west—Chenal, Pleasant Valley, St. Charles (where my son lives), almost entirely White.

I suppose it's a sign of progress that the transition process has slowed considerably from three decades ago when a single Black family moving into a White block would cause panicked flight. Black families have lived in our neighborhood for years, one or two more every year, and no forest of for sale signs has gone up on White lawns. Of course, it must be acknowledged that those mostly White enclaves farther west are very expensive. How many of my White neighbors could move there if they wanted to?

What about my wife and me? The house next door on the north is owned by a young White couple and their baby, so I think we're "safe" there, but the elderly couple on our south, the woman not in good health, that big yard to take care of—what would we do if they moved out and a Black family moved in? Coincidentally, we've been talking about downsizing lately anyway, so . . ..

*

Retired now, I've fallen into a routine of going to the local McDonald's in the morning to drink coffee and swap lies with the other old timers there; most afternoons I go to Burger King and drink Diet Coke and read. A full life, hey? Virtually everyone who works in both restaurants is Black. I know most of them by sight, and they know me, and we're cordial to one another, sometimes chat briefly and even joke. I'll speak of "my friends" at McDonald's and Burger King to my wife, and she'll know whom I'm talking about. True, sometimes she'll roll her eyes, but not always.

One day she and I were walking in our neighborhood when a car passed us, horn blaring. I glanced over long enough to see a young Black man waving and hollering something. That sort of messing with the old folks is not unusual for teenagers. *Hey, why are you still alive, you ridiculous old farts!* With a young Black person, that razzing the old White couple carries an element of danger. We averted our eyes, kept on walking. A few seconds later, the car disappearing over the hill, thinking about that smiling Black face, I realized that he was one of my "friends" from Burger King.

*

So what's the point of all this? Am I implying that my experience is universal (or, more properly, "national"), that my three-score-and-ten represents race relations in this country since World War II, that I *am* White America? Or perhaps the opposite, that I am unique in the breadth and variety of my interactions with people of color, that all ye should look upon me and marvel?

No. I imply nothing. I don't know what the meaning of this is.

*

Include among the many medical and intelligence tests I was subjected to in that delightful process of being inducted into the Army was one in which I was invited to read the number found among mottled shapes on a succession of flash cards. I was cruising along quite nicely until I came to a card with no number on it. "Nothing there," I said to the bored corporal. "Look again." I did. "Nothing," I said. "You're color-blind to green" he said. "No, I can see green just fine," I said.

I can see green—certain shades of green, anyway. But there is a shade of green I see as gray. It wasn't enough to keep me out of the Army, curse the luck, and except for the occasional sartorial embarrassment, I haven't found my mild color-blindness much of a handicap.

There are times, though, when I'll be suddenly . . . I'm not sure what the word is, what the emotion is . . . suddenly bemused or nonplussed or something akin to *worried* to think there's a color out there, a color all around me, that I don't see clearly, see wrong, don't see at all. That doesn't happen often, though. Generally I'm quite content to forget it's there. That worries me, too.

BARBARA SABOL
TENDING

The day was bright and busy
with graveside visitors
generous in the softness
of loss: an offering
to the distraught woman
digging in the dirt
with her hands.

Above-ground, my mother
would have *tsssked*
at my incompetence, arriving
with a box loud with marigolds,
a potted red geranium.
No trowel, no soil, no jug of water.

She might smile now
at my fumbled gesture
of love, my eternal tussle
with the simplest of things.

A supple wind passed once
through the vividness
rooting around her stone,
and I knelt back
on the scuffed earth above her,
finally able to cry.

Sabol

JONATHAN B FERRINI
"THE GOLDEN STATE"

The Department of Motor Vehicles in California is a great equalizer. It has no race, income, gender, or sexual prejudices. It treats everybody miserably. What happened to this state? Rising rents, astronomical home prices, traffic congestion, homelessness. I remember growing up in California in the fifties, life was better. Orange groves lined the freeways. You could hop in the car, and drive across town without it taking hours. It's no longer "the Golden State" I remember. But the one thing that hasn't changed is that the DMV metes out its horrendous experiences equally, to all those unfortunate to endure it. You meet all kinds of people at the DMV. You might call the DMV a "Golden Melting Pot." I'm sitting in a crowded room surrounded by people from throughout the world, who speak languages I can't understand.

I'm sleepy, and can barely keep my eyes open. I was awake all night worried that I may fail the driving test due to my age, and poor vision. I've got to renew my license. It's my independence. I've been driving since I was sixteen. I wish I had Didi here to comfort me. Didi was my wife of fifty years who passed recently. She was always at my side, through "thick and thin." If I get my license renewed, I'm still relevant. I'm an old man, a "dinosaur" nobody cares about, and, without my driver's license, I'm helpless.

It's so crowded I was lucky to find a chair next to a young Asian woman, dressed in business attire, with her eyes glued to her "smart phone." I could tell from her wardrobe, she was refined, educated, and felt out of sorts within the DMV. She looked very organized; the type of person whose life has gone according to plan. She sat next to a buff, twenty-something, Latino male with a large tattoo on his forearm. He looked like a gang member. On her other side, sat a tall, skinny, "White-trash" looking kid, who resembled a dope addict.

I'm staring up at a monitor waiting for my number "82637" to be called. It will be hours before it's called.

My long wait passed by listening to the conversation between the three young people seated near me. We had one thing in common; we were native sons and daughters of the Golden State at the mercy of the DMV. Friday morning slowly crept into afternoon as we waited for our numbers to be called.

The tall, skinny kid, introduced himself as "Timmy," to the young

Latino, and asked about the tattoo on his forearm. The young Latino said, "The tattoo on my forearm reads, 'El Chico de Ajo' which translates into 'Garlic Boy.' I've gone by the name "Garlic Boy" for many years now." The young Asian woman pretended to be preoccupied with her smart phone as the two spoke.

Garlic Boy told his story to Timmy. "The screams and cries are loudest at night, and aggravate the inmates who encourage the predators, and fantasize about the fate of the prey. I chant 'Om Mani Padme Hum,' and peace, replaces terror. I chanted every night after being incarcerated at Corcoran State prison for five years.

"Soon after my incarceration, I visited the prison library, and randomly selected, 'The Teachings of Buddha.' Reading it removed the hatred and vengeance consuming me.

"Gilroy California is a farming community known for growing garlic. Our family lived in a trailer home located downwind from a garlic processing plant, which gave my family the permanent stench of garlic.

"There are two social classes who live and work in Gilroy: wealthy landowners tracing their lineage to Spanish land grants, and migrant farm workers harvesting their crops."

Timmy asked, "How did you end up in prison?"

"Gilroy can get hot in the summer. My parents sent me to purchase a few groceries. I entered the town minimarket, and dashed for the Slurpee machine to cool off. I poured a tall Slurpee, and grabbed the groceries. As I approached the counter to pay, a Latino gang entered the store which was empty except for me and Ernesto, the proprietor. One gang member stood guard at the entrance.

"The leader of the gang smelled my garlic stench, placed his arm around me saying, 'You're my garlic boy.' His grip was firm, and he approached the counter with me in tow. He held a gun to Ernesto's head demanding money. Ernesto opened the register, and handed over the money, begging, 'Please don't kill me!' The gunman turned to me, and said, 'You stink man!' He hit me on the back of the head with the butt of the gun. I fell unconscious.

"I was falsely accused of being a member of the gang robbing the minimarket. The public defender ignored my plea of 'wrong place, wrong time,' and pressured me to accept a plea deal. I was sentenced to prison, and Ernesto was elected mayor of Gilroy on a 'law and order' campaign.

"When I was paroled, the bus ride home from prison felt like a prison cell as it crawled up Interstate 5 surrounded by Central Valley farms. I'm anxious, and clutch the 'Teachings of Buddha.' I silently chant, 'Om

Mani Padme Hum,' which calmed me. I got off the bus at Ernesto's minimarket to buy a bottle of champagne to celebrate our family reunion, and treat myself to a Slurpee which I dreamed about in prison.

"The bus stopped in front of the minimarket. I entered, and recognized Ernesto behind the counter. I poured a Slurpee, and selected a bottle of champagne. I approached the register, and asked Ernesto, 'Remember me?' to which he replied, 'No. You all look alike!' The doors to the minimarket swung open, and in the store mirror behind Ernesto, I see the 'shark like' stare of a 'meth head' quickly approaching the register, determined to rob, and likely kill Ernesto. I turned to the meth head, rolling up my shirt sleeve, revealing prison 'tats' criminals recognize, while giving him my 'prison eye stare down.' I held the bottle of champagne like a baton. The meth head stops dead in his tracks saying, 'It's cool man. No hassle from me!' He backs his way out of the store, and runs to his car speeding away. Ernesto knew he 'dodged a bullet,' and held out his hand to shake, saying, 'Thank you. How can I repay you?' I hand him my copy of 'The Teachings of Buddha.' I walked out of the store to my family reunion, sipping the Slurpee like expensive cognac."

Garlic Boy's experience in the minimarket brought back an old memory I shared, "We owned a corner grocery store and lived in an apartment upstairs. We knew all our customers by name. I put two sons through college with that corner market. We were forced out of business by a supermarket which opened across the street."

Timmy spoke next.

"I grew up in the high desert of Southern California. It's sun-scorched, flat, and runs along Interstate 15 towards Vegas. Trailer home and apartment rents are low. The major industry in the area is meth production. Dad split leaving me and mom to fend for ourselves. Mom graduated from alcohol to opiates to heroin, and couldn't raise me. My aunt and uncle filed papers to assume my custody, motivated by the specter of being paid by the county as foster parents. They sobered up long enough to pass muster by the county. We lived in a beat up, prefabricated home, on a large plot of worthless, desert land, with no neighbors. My aunt and uncle were stoned most of the time. My dinner was fast food, a can of chili, or frozen dinners.

"I'm assigned to a county road crew picking up trash along the interstate highway wearing an orange vest and helmet. There are four of us on the crew who live in halfway homes and are required to work until our probation periods expire.

"Our boss is Deputy Horace who drives the orange county van

which tows a trailer, including our portable plastic toilet. He is tough. Regulations require we get a one-hour lunch, and two, 15-minute breaks, but Horace only gives us a half hour to eat the unappetizing county-provided sack lunch. The smug deputy is nearing retirement, and never leaves the van with the air conditioning roaring.

"The trash we pick up along the highway symbolizes lives gone haywire. Most of it is cans, bottles, fast food packaging, and condoms, but today we found a weathered photo album, and a baby doll. The photo album depicted a happy family I envied, and I wondered what had befallen them. I spied a used hypodermic needle which reminded me of my mom who died of a heroin overdose while I was in prison."

Garlic Boy asked, "You did time too, my man. What crime did you do?"

"My aunt's husband, Brady, drove a sewage truck for thirty years. His job was to pump sewage from portable toilets, and clean out the filthy, plastic bathroom enclosures.

"On my eighteenth birthday, I was given a birthday present of sorts. I was handed the key to the sewage truck, and told that it was now registered in my name. Brady wanted me to drive the truck to Los Angeles, Las Vegas, and then to Nogales, making a stop in each city, while unknown people attended to the sewage tank.

"I was arrested at a state agricultural inspection station when x-ray equipment alerted officers to the hidden compartments Brady constructed in the sewage tank, which he packed with meth. I was facing a forty-year sentence for interstate transfer of narcotics. The US attorney was a kind, middle-aged woman. She offered me a plea deal if I flipped on Brady. I wouldn't rat because my aunt and uncle would cut mom off from her heroin. I was a first-time offender, and the US attorney knew I was protecting my mother. She took pity on me, and recommended to the judge I receive the minimum five-year sentence."

Garlic Boy empathized with Timmy, and asked, "How's probation?"

"It's a dangerous job working alongside the busy highways. Drivers routinely throw garbage at us. The people racing by us have contempt, pity, or sadistic pleasure for our plight, and, are dangerously glued to their cell phones.

"Our crew came upon a smelly trash bag. It wasn't uncommon to find decaying pets but as we examined the bag, it split open, revealing a stillborn baby girl. The sight of that baby really freaked me out. My childhood, and the road crew job, was like moving through the stages of purgatory, and, the final stage before entering hell, was finding a baby in a trash bag. We were ordered by Deputy Horace to bury her alongside the highway, to avoid 'paperwork' and 'demerits.'

"I was ready to end my misery, and take Deputy Horace with me, when I heard a tire blow out, and noticed an out of control semi-truck heading towards our crew, which would kill us all. I warned my crew members who dashed into a culvert for safety. I knew Deputy Horace wouldn't hear the warning horn with his windows closed, air conditioning running, and his playlist blasting from the van speakers. My finger quivered on the trigger of the warning horn, but I decided to warn Deputy Horace in time for him to run for safety. The fat old deputy soiled his pants, vomited, and passed out in the culvert. He was breathing and scared into unconsciousness.

"We discarded our orange vests and helmets, wandering down the highway, towards a fate unknown."

I felt sorry for Timmy. I looked over at the young Asian woman who appeared to wipe a tear from her eye, and Garlic Boy was sullen.

Timmy and Garlic Boy suffered as young men. I reminded them, "Learn from your mistakes and make hay while the sun shines." Timmy reached for his 'smart phone' and began punching away at it. They call it "texting." I don't know what the future holds for these young people, but I wouldn't want to be young today. Who needs instant communication, and multiple methods of sending a written message, or a photo? Nobody wants to have a conversation anymore. Doesn't anybody ever pick up the phone anymore?

My old smoker's cough flared up, and I tried my best to suppress it. If I went outside to cough, I would lose my seat. The young Asian woman reached into her fashionable handbag, pulled out a box of throat lozenges, saying, "Hello, Sir, I'm Amy Lum. My grandmother, Lao Lao, always found these helpful for a cough." I was impressed with the young woman's manners, and mention of her grandmother. I introduced myself, "Hello, Amy. I'm Maury." I returned the box to Amy who motioned to Garlic Boy, and Timmy, to help themselves to a throat lozenge.

The shy, silent, young woman felt a simpatico with Garlic Boy and Timmy. Amy introduced herself to Garlic Boy and Timmy, "My name is Amy Lum. I couldn't help but overhear your stories and I feel sympathy for both of you.

"I also had a tough time as a young woman. I leaned over the railing of the Golden Gate Bridge staring at the choppy waters below, wondering about the many poor souls who jumped to their deaths, and tried to relate to the pain they suffered. I was disappointed knowing that all my hard work didn't result in my admittance to any of the professional schools to which I applied. It was the first time I knew failure, but it wasn't worth jumping to my death.

"My guidance counselor suggested that I may be the victim of admission discrimination against the large number of highly qualified Asian students applying to professional schools.

"Instead, I accepted the fact that 'I didn't try hard enough' or, 'I wasn't good enough.'

"My position in the middle of the bridge, deciding whether to turn back to San Francisco, or travel to Marin County, was a metaphor for my straddling two cultures, Chinese and American.

"I grew up within the affluent city of Burlingame on the San Francisco Peninsula, about twenty minutes from downtown San Francisco. I was the only daughter of successful Chinese American parents. Both parents were overachievers, and expected the same from me. I didn't disappoint them. When I set a goal, I never failed to attain it. I felt invincible, and believed anything was possible, if I put my mind to it.

"I was admitted to my first college choice, Berkeley. I joined an elite sorority, 'Chi Nu Album,' also known as 'CNA,' which consisted of the daughters of the Bay Area elite. I was a devoted and reliable sorority sister, rising to the prominent position of president of CNA, because I always got things done. CNA was instrumental in welcoming me into the privileged, Caucasian lives of my sorority sisters, which made me distance myself from my Chinese cultural roots. It may have been self-loathing, but I just didn't want to feel different.

"I was the only Asian member of the sorority, and, its first Asian president. It was my habit since childhood to make friends with the Caucasian children of the affluent, always wanting to fit in with my Caucasian friends.

"I successfully completed a double major in U.S. history and biology at Berkeley, setting my sights on a career as a patent lawyer specializing in medical-related intellectual property.

"My parents were caught up in the grind of the daily life of American professionals. They abandoned their cultural identity, unable to pass on Chinese traditions to me, leaving it to my grandmother, Lao Lao. They felt guilty for being too busy to be hands-on parents, and showered me with gifts, and money, to assuage their guilt.

"Lao Lao attempted to instill in me our rich Chinese heritage, and teach me to speak Mandarin. I didn't understand the language, and the

Chinese traditions were unfamiliar to me, so, I gravitated away from my heritage, choosing to 'fit in' with my Caucasian friends.

"Lao Lao suggested that we visit 'Angel Island' which was formerly a detention center for mostly Chinese immigrants. It's adjacent to Alcatraz, but might as well be Alcatraz. Conditions for the detainees were horrible, and many immigrants spent years on the island. Visiting Angel Island made my disappointments feel small in comparison to their plights.

"I no longer wanted to straddle two cultures. Leaving Angel Island, a flock of sea birds flew over the ferry boat, and Lao Lao said, 'Look, my dear granddaughter. It's the angels flying over to say goodbye, and thank you for visiting.' I thought to myself that perhaps the sea birds were the souls of the immigrants. As the ferry boat moved further from the island, I looked towards the Golden Gate Bridge, eager to embrace my Chinese ancestry with the help of Lao Lao.

"I gained strength and determination from the immigrants I met on Angel Island. I'm grateful to the proud souls who shared our visit to Angel Island. What appeared to be a life-changing setback for me as a young college graduate was actually an invitation to learn my heritage, and discover my life's purpose. I found a position as an intern at the 'Asian Pacific Islander Law Center,' where I quickly rose through the ranks into a paid position, after devising a student outreach program for Asian students without a connection to their culture. I finished law school at night, passed the bar exam, and devote my law practice to Asian and Pacific Islander legal defense.'

I suspected Timmy and Garlic Boy, like myself, couldn't relate to Amy's privileged upbringing, and academic disappointments, but we could all relate to Amy's cultural identity challenges. It didn't matter whether we were the children of farm workers, the White, "working poor," or the Jewish grocer within a predominately White, Christian neighborhood. We all knew what it was like to be "on the outside, looking in," as Amy envied, and sought eagerly, to mimic the lives of her well-to-do Caucasian classmates. I admired Amy's resolve not be beaten by her disappointments, applauded her perseverance, and was happy to see her succeed. I provided Amy, Timmy, and Garlic Boy the lesson I learned long ago, "Life spares no pain and disappointment to anybody, much like the DMV." I sadly, added, "Most of the time, I feel all alone. I wish my sons would call me more often." I fell asleep.

I was awakened by Amy, whispering, "Wake up, Maury. They called your number. We're rooting for you."

Like a Buddhist monk, Garlic Boy calmly said, "Wish it so, Maury, and it will be."

Timmy said, "You'll ace the exam, Maury."

I approached the counter behind which sat, an African American woman. She looked like a career DMV employee, approaching retirement age, and gave me the impression she was a "by the book" and "tough as nails" DMV examiner. She told me to look into a vision testing machine, and repeat the symbols, letters, and numbers I saw. I struggled. She appeared impatient. "I just can't do it," I exclaimed. It was late in the afternoon when I learned that I failed the vision test and was told my license wouldn't be renewed. I was dejected. I turned to exit from the counter, but heard, "Sir, why don't you place some cool, moist, napkins on your eyes. You'll find them in the men's room. Come back in thirty minutes. You may try again."

I returned to the counter, but struggled again with the vision charts. I believed I flunked the test a second time. The "tough as nails" DMV employee, said, "You passed!" I was elated, and wanted to kiss her. She smiled, and said, "My grandmother always recommended cool, moist, compresses as a cure for the blues. Never failed me yet! They didn't fail you, either. Your new license will arrive in the mail within sixty days."

I was so happy; I could dance out of the building. I wanted to share my good fortune with my three new friends, but they were gone, vanished like a "Santa Ana Wind" into The Golden State. I was impressed by the youth of California after meeting Amy, Garlic Boy, and Timmy. Despite their diverse backgrounds, I believe, if anybody can fix California, making it truly "Golden" for everybody, it will be young people like them. A day at the DMV taught me: "The Golden State" is a state of mind.

WILLIAM OGDEN HAYNES
TRADING UP

That Monday morning, he saw the future, clear and true as a diamond.
He was a nonentity, living through a never-ending, monotonous, reiteration
of days. It was time to go to work, but he stood unhurried in the shower,
thinking about the last ten years. He remembers, in high school, everyone
said, "You'd better go to college or you'll end up in trade school." So, he
earned good grades, a bachelor's degree, and had great expectations.
But, for the last five years, he'd been earning just enough money to get
by, entering data into the computer system of a large corporation. It was
one of those jobs where raises, vacations and promotions were few and
far between. There was no fulfillment, ownership, or investment in the
work. It was the morning he decided that he wouldn't go in to the office,
not this Monday, or ever again.

And he wasn't alone. That morning, from the window of his midtown
apartment, he looked down on the masses of swirling, slumberous forms,
in the sweaty hothouse city, as they lumbered toward their jobs. Dreamily,
they walked toward the cars, busses and subways that took them to work.
Like his, many of their jobs were spine-breaking, mind-numbing, dead-end,
soul-sucking, blind-alleys. That day, he didn't ride the crowded elevator
that rose like vomit inside the skyscraper, stopping at each successive floor
where workers spewed out into the hallway and flowed to their cubicles.
It was a day he wouldn't sit with a keyboard and mouse, transducing
his dreams into pixels on a flat-screen monitor, to power a dystopian
scheme, run by and for the one-percent. Instead, that Monday, he was
off to class at a technical school to learn a trade, a craft that's important,
where he could take pride in his work and earn a fair wage.

Four years later, in the same city, the man lies in a cool, dark, crawlspace
lit by a flashlight. He's re-plumbing a beautiful old home in the historic district,
replacing rusty galvanized pipes with copper. He twirls the pipe cutter, carefully
polishes each copper piece with steel wool, applies the flux, sweats every joint
with a propane torch, touches it with the unfurled rope of solder, watching it
smoke and bubble. And as he waits for the joint to cool, he recalls the day
years ago, that he deserted a cubicle to learn a trade. The day he leapt from
the toneless, tiresome, treadmill and recaptured his soul. It was a Monday
morning, when he saw the future, clear and true as a diamond.

Haynes

HOPE

The Country Café is a small restaurant five miles outside a two
stoplight town in south Alabama. There are living quarters out back
where Sharon, who is the owner, cook and waitress, resides with

Gizmo her cat. All she has to her name is the café, three ramshackle
rooms, and a 2010 Ford Focus with two-hundred thousand miles on it.
She's never had good luck with men. Her first husband left with another

woman, the second was abusive and the last one died in Afghanistan.
And out here in the country, there are precious few chances to meet
someone, even though she'd like to. Sometimes, she thinks about

selling this place and getting a job in Atlanta, but right now she has
no time to dwell on such thoughts. Today, even though business is slow,
she has a regular customer sitting at a table outside, waiting for service.

The café patio is a small slab of cracked concrete hemmed by weeds.
The tubular furniture is coated with mildew and rust, but the vinyl
webbing is still comfortable. The round mesh metal tables are skewered

in the center by poles holding faded red canvas umbrellas, ragged from
age and the sibilant wind blowing across the farmland. This afternoon,
the sole customer on the patio is a man with three days growth of beard,

a University of Alabama hat and a pocket full of money from a recently
cashed paycheck. He comes here every Friday, and sits at the same table,
cuddling his beer, watching the sun slowly descend over the cow pasture

across county road fifty-one. She knows this man will order a cheeseburger
and fries and not leave until he downs at least three Budweisers. As he
finishes his lunch and second beer, he daydreams, watching two flies

buzz over a spatter of ketchup on his empty plate. Before she
takes his last beer out to the patio, she looks at her dim reflection
in the stainless steel ice machine, straightens her hair, and smooths

(cont)

her apron. They talk while she clears the table, and he finally says,
"You know Sharon, if I keep comin' out here, maybe someday you'll
go to the movies with me." And then he takes off his hat, and like

Andy Griffith, gives her one of his broad, gap-toothed, hayseed grins.
As she walks back inside, she marvels at how little it takes to give
a person hope, and that for her, little may actually be enough.

Haynes

TAKING A CHANCE ON HAPPY HOUR

For my afternoon cocktail, I almost switched from a Manhattan
to bourbon and water, because I found that sweet vermouth had
4 grams of carbohydrates per ounce, and two Bing cherries add
2.8 grams more. That's about half the carbs that the Atkins Diet

says we can have in an entire day. It would be sad indeed to see
myself relinquish a drink I have always loved for a watered-down
Kentucky brown. So, I'm sticking with my Manhattan. But, as I
look at my drink cooling in its glass on the coffee table, I believe

I see the carbs, from just that one ounce of vermouth, teeming like
bacteria in a Petri dish. They all wear little carbo-smiles and waggle
their tails in anticipation, like spermatozoa on their trek to fertilize
an egg. They would love to see me balloon up like a pregnant woman

so my pants are tight, and I hyperventilate scaling a flight of stairs.
They would revel in seeing me at Dillard's buying yet another set of
fat clothes or surfing the web for a foolproof new fad diet. I know
the carb count is not high in vermouth and cherries, but it would be

just my luck that it is sufficient to put a monkey wrench in my
fat-burning engine. And that would make me depressed, as I stand
naked on my new electronic scale displaying changes in weight
and percent body fat. Even if I keep my hand gently poised on the

adjacent towel bar to cheat the scale, the screen may reveal a grim
portrait of excess weight and coronary risk. And if I don't jump off
the scale before it sends its signal, I will weep as it transmits
my new numbers through WIFI, to an app that adds them to a graph, (cont)

hopelessly flat-lined or trending in the wrong direction. And even
if all that comes to pass, when happy hour rolls around, I like to think
I will occasionally drink a toast with my keto-unfriendly Manhattan.
Cheers to all you carbohydrates, morph into glucose, burn in hell.

Haynes

BLACKFACE

. . . the anonymity that catalog sales offered was a powerful corrective to the
abuses of the Jim Crow era. This idea of delivering anything to anyone,
anywhere, was selling social justice at a time when segregation and racism
severely restricted the rights, as well as shopping habits, of Black Americans.
"How Sears Kit Homes Changed Housing,"
Patrick Sisson, curbed.com, October 2018.

On a cool autumn evening in 1985, an old man in a red watch cap
and flannel shirt sits reminiscing on a lawn chair in his back yard. He
was lucky to start working at a foundry in his youth, a job most Black
men then could never attain. When his White co-workers saw his humor

and work ethic, they accepted him as a friend. After all, with their faces
covered in soot, all the men looked the same. He takes a deep draw on a
long-neck bottle of Miller beer, balanced precariously on the night-wet
grass. He thinks back almost fifty years to 1940, when he spent his savings

to build a house on this lot he inherited from his father. The bungalow
was sold as a kit by Sears and Roebuck. It came to town by rail with over
30,000 parts, and he remembers the day it was delivered on two flatbed
trucks from the train station. Over many weeks and cases of beer, he and

his friends from the foundry assembled it on late afternoons, after working
all day in front of a furnace. His wife made sandwiches in the back seat of
their 1935 Packard, and the workers shuffled back and forth between the car
and their scaffolds. The men came to the site directly from the foundry,

covered with charcoal, soot and dust, faces black, like chimney sweeps
transformed into carpenters. Curious neighbors watched from afar, but
didn't come over to speak. After all, the town had three foundries, thousands
of employees, and many took second jobs in construction to earn extra

(cont)

income. All the neighbors saw was a bunch of filthy foundry-men
building a bungalow. On the day the house was finished, he took a long
bath, cleaning off all the soot from the foundry. He looked at himself
in the mirror in his church clothes, finally a proud homeowner. His

father would have been pleased. He walked to each house on the block,
with an invitation to celebrate, but nobody came to the housewarming.
He was coolly received, not given the welcome routinely afforded a
foundry-man, just because his face remained black beneath the grime.

Haynes

STILL LIFE ON PLYWOOD

All the houses on this model railway have doors that never open. Yet, each casts
warm light through windowpanes onto the snowbanks, as never-seen occupants enjoy
shelter from the cold. We imagine families happy and content in their beds under
comforters, slippers close at hand, with glasses of water on bedside tables. Perhaps

there's the glow of a fireplace even though no smoke rises up the chimneys. But
not everyone here is happy. There's a man who lives in a house near a white water
tower that stands like a child's rattle at the town limit. He finds this existence
tedious and detests constantly staying at home. When he looks out his window

he sees everything rooted, riveted, and petrified. In this town, the diner is always
open, welcoming anyone who lives in town or gets off the train. But here, people
never leave their houses and the train rarely stops. Even then, no one gets on or off.
There are a church, five small shops, a fire department and a police station, but no

crimes or fires ever occur. The only shoppers are frozen in their stride on the
sidewalks in front of the stores. Automobiles on the streets are immobile, going
somewhere, but nowhere. Some cars sit anchored at railroad crossings, endlessly
watching the signals burn red, and then extinguish as the safety gates rise and fall.

A man in a green wool coat is frozen in time as he lifts a crate from the bed of
his pickup truck to the loading dock at the train station. Electrical poles line
the thoroughfares and the street lights are constantly on, as if there was everlasting
night. In this town, it's always winter. There is snow on every roof, and pine trees

(cont)

poke up through drifts that never melt. There's a boy on a sled stopped halfway down a snow-covered slope, his candy cane muffler defying gravity as it waves motionless behind him. And as the train approaches the edge of town, the same glassy stare of a deer standing in the darkness beneath a northern pine is always

caught in the headlight. The man who lives by the water tower is tired of the stillness and repetition. He dreams about waking up one morning, opening the front door, trudging through foot-deep snow to the depot, on a day when the train will actually stop. He'll walk by all the inanimate figures on the sidewalk

and past the stationary man unloading the crate from his pickup. The door of the train will open and he'll climb three steps into the empty passenger car. And as the train slowly pulls away, he'll begin to worry. He'll wonder if once aboard, the train will ever stop again to let him get off. But even if he could

disembark, there's a fact that has never crossed his mind: As he rides this model railroad, the town he's headed for will always be the one he left behind.

Haynes

TOM KROPP
FEROCIOUS FOXY

Through no fault of her own, Jane was almost fired on her first day in India as the rich family's dog babysitter and walker.

"Foxy! You little shit! No!" Jane shouted as the small dog bounded out of her bag and dashed down the park path. Foxy had picked her prey and pounced like a panther on the unsuspecting monkey tamely eating what the kids were offering. Foxy's gaping maw engulfed the money's neck. Her needle-like teeth sliced and diced bones and tissue, almost decapitating the poor mangled monkey. Foxy savagely shook her head, mauling the monkey with serious satisfaction.

The kindergarten class of kids screamed in horror at the slaughter occurring quite close to them. A lady teacher tried to act heroically by shouting and waving her hands at Foxy, hoping to make her drop the monkey. Foxy growled around the morsel in her mouth.

Foxy saw Jane coming and darted away. Foxy was new in town and sick of all the cows that were allowed to wander freely amongst traffic and people. Foxy was kicked at by a cow. She dropped the monkey and attacked the back leg of the kicking cow. Foxy's little fangs fastened on the cow's high, hind leg and it bellowed in pain, "Mooooo!"

The cow catapulted forward crashing into more cows. They followed herd etiquette by stampeding and bellowing. They bulldogged by bodies, bashing, smashing, and stampeding some folks on foot. The herd collided with an elephant and he joined the mad melee of fleeing cattle. Cars swerved, stopped, clashed, and crashed. Pedestrians shouted and screamed, along with cursing.

Jane knew her job was at stake and stayed on the chase. She followed Foxy's wake of destruction with many people injured with bruises, broken bones, and cuts, but luckily no deaths. Suddenly Jane encountered Foxy and she dipped down, grabbing the fanged and fierce little munchkin demon, stuffing her back in her carry bag. Pandora's box came to mind.

She ducked in some brush where she paused and panted while studying her client's terrible terrier. Jane was shaking like a drunk in detox as her heart hammered hard. Now the demented dog was happy, wagging her tail, and seemed to be smiling.

"You're a bipolar bitch, Foxy," Jane observed grimly.

Jane realized she shouldn't have been surprised. She got the job under similar circumstances. A week earlier Jane was just another pretty brunette with the summer off college when she saw the internet ad showing a family and dog that needed a dog watcher and housekeeper while on their trip to India and France.

Jane jumped at the job offer. She was headed to the interview when she spotted the family and dog from the ad photo in the park ahead.

"Foxy! No!" They shouted as Foxy spun and slipped her collar before breaking away. She pounced like a puma as her fierce fangs snapped like a trap on a goose's wing. The big bird bravely battled back, swatting Foxy with one wing and jabbing beak stabs at her. The goose's mate honked in horror and rushed to burst in the brawl. It was a blur of flashing, flapping wings and pugnacious pecking beaks while Foxy savagely snapped back, biting both birds.

Jane realized it was her chance to get the job and charged into the fight. Both birds batted her with wing whacks and belligerent beaks banged her body and lacerated limbs. Feathers, fabric, and fur flew from the fight. Jane earned some bloody bites from Foxy as she carried her away like a football while running from the geese honking and chasing her.

Boldly Jane walked to the family's father, Achmed. The geese and dog had torn her clothes and her hair was in wild disarray. She sported bloody bites and bruises with scratches.

    With surprising aplomb, Jane held out Foxy to Achmed.

    "I'm Jane and I'm here about the job," she announced.

    "You got it. You can start today." Achmed spared her a smile.

****

    "There's got to be an easier way to see the world than watching over you," Jane criticized Foxy.

    "Yap! Yap! Yap!" Foxy barked back, as if arguing her side of things.

    "You would say that you crazy little bitch. Let's go home," Jane decided and carried her paymaster's prized pet back towards their temporary home.

NEIL CARPATHIOS
LOVE ACCOUNT

Like savings,
every month I deposit some
for future use.
I'm preparing just in case
one day I wake up empty,
a bitter, lonely man.
I don't want to come across
a puppy on a walk and curse no leash
instead of bending over to pat its furry head.
I don't want to curse my phone
when my children don't call.
Don't want to give the finger
to the mailbox, to the garbage men doing their job,
to my neighbor obsessed with cutting his grass.
That's why I put a little of my love aside.
I have to choose what to love completely,
what to love slightly less.
The full moon like a giant pearl, I love,
but can get away with about 63.5%.

(cont)

My grandson's laugh is harder,
I strain to hold back, say, 10%.
I need to be able to stick my card into a slot
for the love I saved to come out.
You can't withdraw what isn't there.
I try to tell her.
But my wife says she wants 110% every day.

My friend is having a good week.
He eats as though making up for lost meals.
Downs forkfuls of lasagna,
grabs breadsticks he dunks in marinara.
He hardly pauses to speak,
nods his bald head
but he's not really listening.
He notices my eyes amazed, says
"I'm eating for two, me and my tumor."
We laugh.
I picture it inside him, a golf ball with a face,
mouth open wide like a baby bird in a nest.
He knows this doesn't make sense,
he should be starving it
but he'd be starving himself too.
I say "Maybe we should drown it,"
pour us more wine. We drink.
He says "I think it likes that too."
"Is it a boy or a girl? What will you name it?"
I ask. He grins. I grin.
He looks down at his plate, then up into my eyes,
says "Your wife is right, math is dumb"
then with a bony hand he wipes his mouth
with a napkin, says "Spend it. Spend all of it."

Carpathios

LISA MECKEL
SOUTHERN AUSTRALIA
Inventory of a Moment

Crossing the never-ending Nullarbor Plain,
  miles from civilization,
   we ride this day into darkness
    when our bus shudders,
      lurches,
        rolls off
          the road
          in a stall.

Stuck on this limestone desert
  of no trees, no people, no city lights,
   fear rises in the riders of the night.
    Sleepers sleep on.
     Men rise,
      step off the bus,
       nervously light up.
        Toxic smoke
          wreathes the air.

I leave the sleepers, ignore
  the men huddled in their
   safe circle, cigarette tips
    sparking orange,

enter the desert.
  Shadows of mounded saltbush scrub
   surround me.
    Nullarbor's ancient
     Aboriginal spirits
      fill the air.

I gaze up into the night sky

  and stars

   millions of them

    fall into my eyes.

Meckel

VIVIAN LAWRY
RUNNING ON ABOUT MY WEDDING

Although the courtship and engagement were a piece of cake, the wedding threatened my sanity, starting with the dresses—both mine and my attendants'—because my younger sister and I always planned that she would wear my wedding gown (Mom's not being an option because she had been married in a powder blue suit decades out of style by then) but in the event, my sister married in October, just three months before my January date, and she was both taller and thinner than I, and although making the dress shorter was easy, making it bigger took some fancy needlework with gussets and lace and so forth, but my sister and I were determined to share a dress, besides which our parents were struggling to pay for two weddings so close together anyway—not that mine was the only body that required accommodation because my best friend from high school who absolutely had to be in the wedding was four months pregnant, dictating that all the female attendants wear empire style dresses, and given the season, I chose burgundy velvet for the bodice and pink crepe for the skirt and getting the velvet rose hair ornament to match the bodice while dying the satin shoes to match the skirt took three and four tries, respectively, finally coming together a couple of weeks before the wedding, and all along, I had to deal with my mother, who kept wanting my wedding to be a carbon copy of my sister's and when I finally lost my temper and said, "Damn it, Mom! No reception in the church basement!" my dad scolded me, saying among other things that I would not disrespect my mother again, so of course I made a tearful apology, and although we did end up renting a hotel ballroom for the reception that turned out to be a huge hassle when the hotel called—after the invitations for the wedding and reception had been mailed—to tell me the ballroom had been accidentally double booked, and then they offered me the cafeteria instead (complete with glassed-in serving counter, stainless steel tray slide, linoleum tile floor, and bare windows) which I declined so then I hustled to find anything, ending up with a room at a nearby Holiday Inn and a few dozen cards printed with the new reception location for ushers to distribute as they showed people to their seats, and all that was before my future in-laws arrived, sending my mother into a tailspin because my future father-in-law was the vice president of a bank whereas my father was a machinist, and my mother-in-law-to-be wore a mink stole while my mother's best church-going coat was red wool that clashed with the bridesmaids dresses, plus she was hyperaware that all of the future in-laws at the wedding had college degrees while my father had an eighth grade education and Mom had had to leave school after tenth grade—and when mama ain't happy, ain't nobody happy—and I figured everything that could go wrong had, but then the weather did a big turnaround, going from such a mild week that even the mink stole was too hot to a blizzard that began the morning of the wedding, dumping nearly two feet of snow, which kept virtually all of our grad school classmates from coming (given that they lived in the university town some fifty miles away) as well as some relatives who lived closer, because it was still coming down when we went to the church, where we couldn't get close parking spaces because those were all taken, and when we entered the church, the smell of baked beans, ham, coffee, and a dozen other mingled aromas assaulted us and when we went downstairs to change into wedding clothes, we learned that the church seniors were enjoying a potluck dinner, which was a regular event the last Friday of each month, and all I could think was, "What if I had tried to have my reception here?" while hoping the smells wouldn't cling to our clothes, and because the seniors and their food took more than half of the big open space, the wedding party women drew the curtains (typically used to separate one Sunday School class from another) along ceiling tracks and changed in one corner with no big mirror to check appearances while responding to questions and comments from seniors on the far side of the curtains, and when I took my father's arm to walk down the aisle, I was a nervous wreck, actually trembling, and Dad said, "I love you daughter. You know you can still change your mind," so he was obviously expecting the worst but I said everything was fine and thanked my lucky stars that the ceremony itself went off without a hitch, except that so many people who'd said they would come didn't, and many people who attended the ceremony left immediately after, so the reception was sparsely attended and I was actually thankful, for all food and drink had to be supplied by the Holiday Inn at costs beyond our means, and the fewer people who made do with nuts, mints, and a single glass of wine, the better, and I should have known right then that this marriage was doomed.

STEVE DEUTSCH
TILTH

Once,
as we sat in the Skeller,
she joked
that she could
get pregnant from a handshake
and Charming Eddie,
that world-class weasel,
jumped up
and overturned the table—
spilling beer and peanuts—
just to be the first
to shake her hand.
I hated that he
beat me to it.

But that was
long ago—
when we were first-year
medical students
and would recite for each other
the bones of the hand
the nerves of the face
the symptoms of rickets
and mispronunciation
might cause a mouthful
of beer to spray
across the table.

Today, I watch our kids
file into her stark white room
where useless instruments beep
over the rhythmic hump
of the respirator
and where we have known for months
that she has lived too long.

(cont)

The kids are grown now
and scattered like
dandelion puffs.
Together,
for the first time in years,
we pass around
a yellowing photo album—
and pause at a picture
of her in her first white coat,
grinning like a caught-out child
as I reach for her hand.

Deutsch

CHRISTOPHER AMENTA
A CLEAN TOWEL

Natalie's mother said to always keep a clean towel in the trunk, just in case. Then she shuffled into the garage in her bedroom slippers and produced one. She returned to the driver's side window, one hand offering a clean, if ancient, blue and white beach towel and the other cinching her bathrobe tight at the base of her neck. Saying nothing more, she did not stay to watch her daughter drive off but instead went back into the house as the car eased down the drive and turned westward. Highways later, Natalie wished she'd reminded her mother that it was only for now, not forever.

It surprised Natalie how often she used the towel, and every time she did, she would call home to tell her mother.

"I washed the car today and used your towel to dry it. The sun here is so hot you have to dry it right away or you'll get spots all over and how are you?"

"I found a dog running loose in the rain and I sat him on your towel and brought him home to his owners. He wouldn't stop fidgeting and he got water all over the seats. Yes, it rains here but not often and not for very long. No the seats are fine; I dried them out in the garage."

"I brought my lunch to the park to eat with a friend and we sat on your towel. Do you like avocado? Yes you do, it's green and soft and they use it to make guacamole and they put it on *everything* out here. Anyway, Mary Beth and Jim say hello, they're here making dinner, and can I call you back tomorrow morning?"

"I was at work until 11:30 last night and had to close my eyes for a few minutes on the drive home because I was so tired. You know how I am about driving in the dark. Anyway, I used your towel as a pillow. No, it's just this one client, it's not always like this, and anyway I'm off to Cabo on Saturday so I only need to get through the next few days."

And she did tell her mother that she'd brought the towel to the beach for a date, but she didn't say the rest: that they'd lain out on that blue and white towel and watched the sun descend and the evening settle. That, over the lull of the ocean, Natalie whispered that she didn't know. She said she'd never done anything like this before, not on a beach, not with someone she barely knew, and he said he hadn't either. Natalie didn't tell her mother that the word she arrived at was, okay, saying no hadn't even occurred to her. She didn't tell her mother that afterwards, after she dropped him off and went home, she turned off the car and sat in the garage and looked at the towel, sand-covered and unfurled across the passenger seat, and she cried for the things that distance can do to people.

The next day, Natalie called her mother and said, "I brought your towel to the beach with a man I've gone out with one or two times." Her mother listened as she always did and, as she always did, she asked when her daughter was coming home.

BETH BAYLEY
ROCKET UNCLE DELIVERY CO.
Singapore

They wear windbreakers in reverse, backward jackets flapping
and they don't like to ride in the rain, instead
resting their motorbikes under overpasses to wait
out the afternoon storms, the chicken-wing delivery guy and
the McDonald's delivery guy, and while they wait, they watch
the cocooned cars and listen for thunder under wet wheels.
When the rain stops is when they can go, go
all day and deep into the night, grabbing late noodles
at bright hawker centers and collapsing in a rented bed,
dreaming of perpetual motion, a bike ride without end, amen.

Bayley

SHAW PLAZA, BALESTIER
Singapore

Nobody's ever at my favorite theater, which is why it's my favorite,
but I can't believe it will stay open much longer.
There are more squat toilets than seated ones, first of all,
and the smell of durian from the grocery downstairs wafts up through the vents.
Off-brand versions of "Lost in Your Eyes" and "Wake Me Up Before You
    Go-Go"
play before every showing, so awful they become thrilling.

The theater seats are hard and threadbare, squeaking with the slightest shift,
but that doesn't stop the occasional old uncle
from having a nap in the air-conditioning,
snoring through the public service announcements
about climate change, food waste, and diabetes.

I love this theater fiercely.
I love to go alone to a horror matinee,
buying my ticket from the yawning auntie,
choosing my seat and shivering in the frigid air
and sipping my condensed milk coffee in the dark.

Bayley

POSTCARD FROM THE BABY SHOWER
Singapore

When we are born we have every egg,
all the eggs we will ever release,
and a tableful of us sat by the edge of the jungle
to celebrate one with the fullness of child,
the rest of us with varying amounts of eggs,
wombs previously full or never full
or future full or never to be full.
The jungle was behind us, fullness and rot, overripe.
She's fully cooked, someone said to the expectant mom.
You can have some wine now.
A quarter of a glass, ice-cold and citrine-gleaming,
next to the gifts, organic cotton and recycled plastic,

(cont)

and the platters of avocado toast and falafel,
served by a woman whose big hands and deep voice
told another story, maybe no eggs but one of us just the same.

Bayley

LAUREN ELIZABETH
PURPLE DRAGONFLIES

It had taken a decent amount of staring absentmindedly into the distance for a regret to find its way into my mind. Once it was there it dug its claws deep into my brain and refused to move. *Think of a regret you have – what did you learn from it?* The CommonApp prompt and the words I wrote about Danielle underneath glared up at me from the page. I glared back at it and tapped my pencil dramatically on the side of the desk.

It had been a year since she died. Glancing down at my words I could picture a particular moment in her parents' home, when I felt like the world was coming up from underneath me. An overwhelming sea of purple, childish drawings, and dragonflies formed a protective halo around a life-size photo of Danielle's face in the foyer. I should have smiled back at her. I should have felt a sense of bittersweet peace. But I didn't.

"Whatcha writing about?" Maya leaned in towards me, her eyes sliding off her essay and onto my own. Guilt made me reach out and snatch the page away before she could see what I had put down.

"Nothing."

She played a part in that story too. The one about Danielle.

Maya raised her eyebrows at me, but thankfully turned back to her own regret. I kept the page pressed to my chest, crumpled in my hand, and willed the memory to fade. It had been recessed so long that I didn't even know it was there until AP Literature and college essays made me dig it back up again. After a moment, I determinedly spread the essay back down in front of me. *You're having hard time writing*, I told myself, *because it's only been a year*. I stabbed my pencil into the paper; the lead broke off with a pitiful *snap*. I closed my eyes. Saw her lilac casket being lowered into the ground.

Cancer was a horrible thing to die from. Especially at the age of fourteen.

She was always a little off. She was diagnosed with leukemia mere months into her life, so chemotherapy was as natural as breathing to her. Constant hospital visits and longs days of radiation should have ruined her childhood, but in reality it did the exact opposite. Until the day she closed her eyes for the last time, Danielle lived in a state of oblivious innocence. When people were mean to her, she didn't understand. When she was told that she had to start wearing a bra, to be discreet about her developing body, she didn't understand. When I hid my embarrassment of her behind half-hearted excuses and quick exits…she didn't understand. And I was grateful for that.

Next to me, Maya's essay seemed to be coming along fine. She wasn't caught up in a wormhole of memory. If she knew what I was thinking, I wondered if she would feel just as guilty as I did.

Recess in fifth grade consisted of four square. Back in elementary school, my friends and I were quiet—nice girls. We spent our time after lunch out on the blacktop, sharing inside jokes and pegging each other with the same red rubber ball we claimed from the classroom every day. It was a safe group to belong to. I'm sure that's why, every day, Danielle found her way across the playground to us.

Seven years later, I could still feel the heat of embarrassment that rose to my cheeks whenever she approached. The electric purple of her fuzzy North Face jacket was a spot of brightness against the dull grey of the sky during the winter. My friends never complained. They never said a word against her. They didn't have to. Shifting eyes, subtle coughs, and smiles with too much teeth gave away how they truly felt. "Hey Danielle," I said, every time with a nod towards the line to join. Maya would shoot me a frustrated look.

Standing in her home, a short time after her death, and then in the present while struggling to write a college essay, I remembered those four square games. They haunted me, followed around my deepest memories just waiting to be brought to the surface again. No one else seemed to be having this overly dramatic problem. Once again, I found myself glaring at the few words I had written down.

You're not getting into any schools with this crap, they seemed to say.

Despite the pessimistic opinion on what would ultimately decide my fate for the next few years, I turned the essay in. As the bell released us for the day and Maya and the others swapped stories about their creative triumphs, I was still present in the past. My writing had manifested itself into a twisted reality, where I was trapped between the blacktop of Meadow Brook Elementary and a child's funeral. It felt likely that I would be stuck there for a while.

University admissions didn't seem to understand the internal struggle I went through while writing. It took almost four years for me to even grasp that all the pain and guilt I sensed when thinking of Danielle was unnecessary. I wasn't a mean kid. I was just a kid. Danielle was my shadow for a reason. She didn't know that like everyone else, I only wished to fit in and find some version of popularity, because I never let that version of me reach the surface.

In a middle school filled with kids who turned their noses up at the different, our four square games always welcomed her.

There was a time at her wake when my hands legitimately fisted in rage. A boy was there from her year, sobbing. When she was alive, he tormented her. He bullied her because she was a different. And once again, she didn't understand.

I could see her smile. Hear that high-pitched laugh that always began a few seconds too late. *Think of a regret you have – what did you learn from it?* In my head, I ran far away from Danielle when I was younger. I regretted the thoughts that went through my mind. But the difference between me and that boy at the funeral, who wore her purple dragonfly emblem bracelet and cried like he cared was that through every moment, Danielle saw me as a friend.

NICKOLAS DUARTE
STELLA

Faded speedbumps test the shocks.
A hot day but not as hot as normal.
Early sun rays
    caught in cloud waves
    of dust; kicked up
    by pit bulls racing behind a chain link fence.
A fat white man in a Hillis jersey with a Polar Pop;
    Peyton Hillis but not when he was cut by the Giants
        or by the Bucs
        or the Chiefs
        but when he was the *Madden 12* cover player.

(cont)

So much dust kicked up.
Saladitos stuck
    in lemons claw their way into the mouths
    of brown kids on broken bikes.
A meth-head sleeps on a realtor's face.
A pair of busted, blue Chucks run over too many times to know
    find shelter in the shade of a six-inch curb.
A foreclosed middle school better kept than expected glides past;
two fat coyotes gait by with bellies full of lost cats.
When that school was open
    and had eighth grade girls with tummies heavy from unborn babies
    and magazine drives and I had blue-banded braces
    there were Eastside B-K tags on the walls
    but not anymore—
    when everyone left they must have cleaned it all up.
That Philipino family's been here for years;
    scaring off the javelinas scrounging in tipped-over green garbage bins.
An ice cream man drives by
    and a flash of sticky mucas at the bottom of tiny plastic baby bottles
    and melted Sonic the Hedgehog ice cream bars with frozen gum eyes
        that looked in all directions
        at the army brats and dark men with Korean wives
        and that Black kid with bright blue eyes that smell like cat piss every
            time
        we played Shaq Fu and Mario Kart and Golden Eye
        and his brother that taught us how to do gang signs
        and my dad would try to scare me to stay inside
        first with stories of La Llorona
            but then, later, with news reports of drive-bys.
A childhood of tadpoles (and gunshots.)
An American flag flies high over a corner house
    just under it a flag with a Block A and the words "Bear Down!"
Two young Mexican kids play soccer in their backyard
    kicking up so much dust;
their three-year-old sister in just a pink skirt
    carries her four-month-old baby brother.
A Lowe's branded boxed shed in the neighbor's yard.
An old woman tends her garden.

(cont)

The kids yell at her in Spanish.
She laughs and sprays them with water,
even though it's less hot here in autumn.

*Saladitos are plums which are dried, salted and which can also be sweetened with sugar and anise or coated in chili and lime.

*Arizona Javelina. Though some people may call them "cute," Javelinas are arguably rather ugly animals and possess a rather unpleasant odor which is why some people refer to them as "musk hogs."

Duarte

ROCHELLE JEWEL SHAPIRO
OH, RIFLE

Even sober you are loaded.
Your dark metal sparkles like mica. Polished,
the grain of your wooden stock ripples—
an ochre lake a wisher has tossed a pebble into.
Your stock is a hand on a shoulder,
a caress on a jaw. Your front and rear sights
are both forward-looking. Your trigger,
curved just so for an itchy finger.
What a kick your shot for the shooter,
a jolt of the upper back, a head bobble, a release.

I kneel to you, not on one knee, upper arm resting
on it just above the elbow for steadiness. I kneel
to you on both knees, my palms together.
I kneel to implore you not to aim at children,
at the unarmed. I kneel to you
as I do at my granddaughter's bedside
during her nightmares when I claim,
Shh, you are safe.

Shapiro

BACK-FRONT-DOOR

How rosy for the little girl who dashed up
the front porch and saw her grandfather
dozing, his head dove-like on his shoulder,
hearing his snores whistle out in tweedly puffs.

How lemony her grandmother's homemade polish
that turned mahogany to mirror, and Sophie Tucker wailing
"The Last of the Red Hot Mamas"
on the RCA Victrola, her grandmother
wearing a flowery housecoat and bifocals low
on her thin nose, rasping along.

How quicksilver, this apartment-girl
raced out the back door, round to the front,
and out the back to shut out the echo
of her mother's lampblack childhood stories—
the time her mother whimpered
for a toy circus whip and Grandmother bought it,
yanked her home, and cracked her over the legs
twice, three times, and more, and how her mother
was made to sit on a crate for hours
at the store where Grandmother sold jujubes,
candy buttons on a strip, and Sky Bars.

"Back-front-door," the girl chanted.
"Back-front-door."

Shapiro

BIBBLEBABBLE

Why teach a girl Hebrew
when a woman wouldn't be permitted
to say Kaddish for him,
as her brother someday would?
While your father's voice intoned
over you like God's,
you twiddled the silky fringe of his tallit,

(cont)

in your small fingers,
tickled your palm with it,
braided and unbraided
its strands, and ran
your hand
over his velvet tallit bag,
the deep blue velvet
darkening
in one direction,
paling in the other.

Shapiro

FALLEN HAIR

The blower stirs
wet curls eddying in autumn wind.
Smells like burnt toast.
Hair does not grow after death.
The skin retracts,
making it seem as if it's still growing.
The Nazis wove blankets and linings
for the jackets of uniforms from Jewish hair.

Shapiro

I LOVE YOU LIKE GERMAN BLACK FOREST CAKE
(for my husband on our 51st anniversary)

The ooze of whipped cream
and spongy *Schokolade*, the squish
of pitted cherries with their gleam,
foam lapping like a wave
in a Hokusai woodcut that comes alive,
Ich liebe.

O, the deliciousness of lying entwined
with you on the moist bottom of the Black Forest,
light shafting between the silver firs,
striping us like prisoners

(cont)

of this aphrodisiac spiked
with *kirschwasser.*

Just saying the throaty name,
Schwarzwälder Kirschtorte,
makes me coo
Mein mann, ich liebe dich.
Like a German Black Forest Cake,
I love you.

Shapiro

GAIL LANGSTROTH
BLUE INDESTRUCTIBLE

Two summers ago I moved in.
My neighbor's discarded toilet
hasn't moved—

propped against her alley fence
as if to stop pickets from falling,
I name it *Blue Indestructible.*

She says she wants to get rid of it,
but hasn't found—.
I don't mind.

I like it.

Strategically placed in her open-air
backyard, the toilet is stable, predictable,
accepts any vine, moss, mold.

I call it *Art* and I will miss it.

I will miss my neighbor:

(cont)

our chats, talk of church, her heart,
swollen ankles, diabetes, her love of song.

A friend pulls up in a black SUV and honks,
my neighbor closes her wreath-hung door,
wiggles past the sharp snap of her screen

and waves, *Going to Bible study.*

Her sequined ball cap matches
the hot-pink corsage pinned to her jacket.
Dolled up like that, I say, *you want me to believe: church?*

I'm glad she couldn't find anyone
to cart the toilet away. I'm glad.
I will miss my neighbor.

I move out in 21 days.

Langstroth

MADELINE WISE
THE SCRATCH BIN

They knew better but they did it anyway. Not for the first time, the pre-teen girls, cousin-friends, sneaked into the cow barn (in the quiet of mid-day on their grandparents' farm) raised the bin's lid, and one leg at a time, climbed over the side and dropped into the chicken scratch. Their grandma, Ma, who fed the chickens, would not come for a bucket of scratch until late afternoon, which meant the girls had plenty of time.

Slipping off their shoes and socks, they sat with pleasured grins and moved their bare feet through scratch, sifted it through their fingers, filled the cuffs of their jeans, their shirt pockets and socks. Dust rose from the bin, filmed the air and made them cough a little. They stood and stomped deep into the scratch—the feeling between their toes something like sand or mud. The girls' movements brought a quiet, dry sound of tumbling kernels. The kernels looked like popcorn, but in their mouths, were tasteless rocks and the girls spat them out.

In their own world for a long while, or so it seemed, the girls played, giggled and kept their voices low—their only restraint. From time to time the older girl, taller and acting as a lookout, would stand, lean forward, peer through the barn door and say, "The coast is clear."

Then, suddenly the coast was not clear and she froze with disbelief. A big man in bib overalls, their grandpa, Pa, was sauntering down the narrow sidewalk that stretched between the milk house and the barn. "It's Pa," the lookout whispered. "Pa's coming. I don't think he saw me, but...."

Slowly, carefully, they lowered the wooden lid and said nothing. They tried to ignore their hearts bouncing against their rib cages, and tried not to breathe as they listened to Pa's footsteps. They did not know where he was. His footsteps stopped. He would sometimes lean against the scratch bin and smoke his corncob pipe. Where was he now? Had he heard their voices? Did he suspect that they were in the barn? Did he notice dust motes in sunshine streaming through the windows?

They waited and waited and waited in the dark bin, breathing dust—dust that always rose from playing in scratch except that with the lid down, they breathed heat and dust in silence. Silence was a given; they did not cough, did not whisper, did not move. What should they do? How long should they stay? Where was Pa? They did not dare raise the lid.

Eventually, after what seemed like endless hours in the dark, dusty scratch bin, they eased its heavy lid open. They glanced left and right. Signaling each other with a finger to their lips, they carefully lifted one leg at a time over the side of the bin and dropped to the floor. With fire drill speed they yanked their socks and shoes on. In their newly found freedom, they escaped the barn leaving no trace behind. *No trace*, meaning not one kernel of scratch remained on the barn floor.

In time to come the cousin-friends would ask themselves what they had been afraid of. What was Pa's wrath? What would it have been? The answer: Just words; simply words. Pa's exasperation expressed (with gestures) and in broken English would have been—*You waste! You leave scratch! Cost money! You make mess—make work! I sweep!*

But the cousin-friends did not hear those words. The secret between them was a pact—*no telling*—because there just could be a next time.

ANTHONY RABY
MODERN POETRY

The world is too much with us,
Wordsworth whispered at the sea.
I simply post it as Facebook status
While watching the TV.

Raby

EVERY WRITER'S FEAR

When is a writing desk
like a raven?
When it softly whispers,
"Nevermore."

Raby

MARISA P CLARK
DÉJÀ-VU

In her easy chair my mother combs
the tangles from the ears
of her toy poodle, Déjà-vu,
while the TV blares full volume
Fox's breaking news of another school
shooting. "F-E," she spells.
"What does that mean?"

I've just survived my nineteenth year
of teaching college English; I've come
to visit from out of state. I'm making breakfast
in the kitchen. "Faith," I enunciate
to her white crown of hair.

"F-E," she spells again, "like Santa Fe.
What does that mean?"

(cont)

I spread orange marmalade
crust to crust on my toast
and raise my voice. "Faith!

She's found a snarl and gives the comb
a yank. Déjà-vu squirms off the chair
and waddles out of reach. "I know
how it's pronounced," she growls.
"What does it mean?" She never turns
to look at me, but I perceive
the tight seam of her frown.

I pour my coffee and grip my plate,
then come around to block the TV screen.
The dog, obese, wags her pompom tail.
"Faith!" I shout. "Faith!" I try to keep
the anger from my tone. Yelling,
no longer grounds for punishment,
has become a way of being heard.

I slowly spell: "F-A-I-T-H!"

"What?" my mother says. Then: "Oh."

I eat my breakfast on the couch,
the poodle begging at my side.
A disgruntled teen has shot his school
to smithereens. The body count
is high. My mother aims
the remote at the TV and sighs,
"There's nothing anyone can do
about all that." She switches on
The Price Is Right.

I swallow a dry bite of toast
and recite, "Thoughts and prayers,
thoughts and prayers," but even if she heard,
she wouldn't listen.

Déjà-vu, hoping for a crumb, pricks
her pretty ears.

Clark

ASH WEDNESDAY

A pastor with a pot of ashes appears
on campus where I work. In need

        of I don't know what—maybe everything—
         I approach. She smudges my forehead

and declares me destined to return
to dust. This is not a day I should be made

        to think of death. Emotions race electric
         along my skin: they and the ash are

all I know of touch. Beside her,
handing out church pamphlets, is a woman

        in a wheelchair. American flags fly
        from the handles. Her name is Ramona.

I met her late last spring, some
ten miles from here. I sat with friends

        at a pizza place, at a table near a window.
         We saw her struggle to roll up

the parking lot of the fast food joint
next door. I went to help. She asked

        for water. I pushed her into Burger King
        and offered her a meal. She knew

just what she wanted. Outside again,
she asked for money. "I don't drink

        or do drugs," she said. She needed shelter
        for the night. I gave her all I had

in cash, fifteen dollars, and pushed her
to the bus stop up the hill. My friends

(cont)

observed the whole exchange. Back then
they thought me kind. Now they've

sloughed off that image of me.
It's true I've created pain for others.

I won't say what I've done. Make it up
if you must. Make it ugly, make it cruel.

Those who claim to know me well
feel free to invent the story of my sin.

My greatest wrong was faith
in long friendship, was faith

we would survive my strike
at hot iron, my shot at not being

alone all my life. Now they aim
to teach me the difference between

solitude and loneliness. There's more
to the story—there always is—but what I want

most to say is that this morning, Ash
Wednesday, on my drive to work, I passed

a funeral home and thought, again,
I should write a will despite my lack

of heirs, and I thought, again, I want
a green burial. They do that here,

in New Mexico: let body blend
into earth. When I was a child, my fear

of death was fear of being devoured
by worms. Now it seems so reasonable,

(cont)

truly desirable: that my body's last act satisfy
another's hunger; that I, who long

> for touch, supply the pleasure
> of being ripped by claw and torn by tooth,

that I nourish crow and coyote,
beetle and buzzard. So let me pray:

> Once safely insensate, may my flesh
> offer up its carrion gifts and come

at last to some good use before
it turns to animal shit. To dust.

Clark

FRANCES KOZIAR
THE YEARS OF MY LIFE

For the first twelve years of my life I was normal.
Thirteen. **One.**
Fourteen. **Two.**
Fifteen. **Three.** I noticed, but everyone was sleep deprived, right? Maybe I just wasn't used to it yet.
Sixteen. **Four.** I was different, and I could no longer deny it. I needed eleven and a half hours of sleep per night: four more hours than other people. That was on the good days.
Seventeen. **Five.** It was the age of late-night parties. When I went I hated myself and the world the morning after. I would have had to go to bed right after dinner to get enough sleep, but that year I refused. I pushed myself to get as little sleep as possible, determined not to waste my life in such a way. I became very good at time management, and my peers called me productive. It was when I was seventeen that I counted back, and realized what was happening.
Eighteen. **Six.** I went to university, and I got tested. I had normal iron, normal thyroid, normal B12. I got a sleep study. Normal. Will it get better? I asked the sleep specialist. He couldn't even lie.

Nineteen. **Seven**. I dropped out of university after the first month of my second year, having made it through my first year with hard-won Bs and no social life to speak of. I hated hearing people talk about how little time they had, when they only needed eight hours of sleep a night. I felt so angry at them, so I turned to denial. I didn't think about normal people, or what my old friends were doing. Most careers were now impossible for me. I moved back in with my parents.

Twenty. **Eight**. I worked as a waitress on the weekends, pretending that was what I wanted to be doing at twenty. My parents began taking me to doctors and specialists, but they had never seen my condition before. *Cumulative Hypersomnia*, I found myself explaining to them, instead.

Twenty-one. **Nine**. I met a girl. She was a janitor at the school I began cleaning part-time when waitressing became too much. I had gotten many responses over the years when I had been forced to tell people of my condition—skepticism, disbelief, suggestions of veganism and optimism— but when Kira asked me out and I told her, she looked at me with sympathetic anguish and realized aloud that I had less life to live. I think I fell in love with her in that moment. I didn't tell her it was getting worse, or that I feared it might be terminal. I had gotten used to never relaxing, to always watching the clock to fit in as much as I could, but Kira taught me how to slow down again. We watched movies and played board games and talked for hours. She could make me forget, and sometimes it made me so happy, but sometimes it ravaged my heart as I thought of everything I would do with her if I had the time.

Twenty-two. **Ten**. I no longer envied other people, but my past. What I would do with only fourteen hours of sleep, I thought, looking back on that one year of university. That had been the last year people had believed I was like them, and I hadn't known how good I had had it then. Kira was gone. I had sent her away, unable to handle that I was holding her back, and that she had a future I couldn't even dream of anymore. I hated her in the end—or maybe she made me hate myself—but I loved her too, and breaking up with her broke me. I stopped working, stopped eating. I volunteered at an animal shelter once a week, and my parents adopted an old cat for me—someone to sleep with. I spent my days alone or with my parents, laughing a lot now because I could either laugh or cry.

Twenty-three. **Eleven**. I wanted to escape my parents' house, and I thought of Kira a lot that year. I might have called her up if I hadn't seen her with a new girlfriend on Facebook. But I knew she wouldn't have taken me back. Anyone who knew the truth would find me depressing. Maybe that's why I smiled so much. I began buying presents for people begging on the street. I pretended my parents' friends were my own.

Twenty-four. **Twelve**. I had just over four hours to spend each day. I looked into suicide, but decided I couldn't give up what time I had left when time was what I wanted most. I began drawing: it didn't take too much time. I drew Rome and Paris and beaches. I drew houses and families and Christmas trees. I drew Sleeping Beauty.

Twenty-five. **Thirteen**. While the lives of other twenty-five-year-olds stretched ahead of them like country roads, mine had ended when I'd left university. Now, I lived in limbo, albeit one packed with to-do lists. My dreams were my one haven, and I started writing stories about them, and about the things that were lent to me so fleetingly in them. I saw Kira again, there, saw a future with her that would never be. Some days my happiest moment was right when I woke up, when I was still between this world and that one, before I'd remembered my life.

Twenty-six. **Fourteen**. I ate my one meal as I speed-walked, waving to neighbours or the street folk I knew, walked quickly as much to get in some exercise to counteract the atrophying of my muscles as because I was always fighting to do as much as possible. I began having one-night stands, one scheduled in each month like everything else. I found the people online. Some weren't that great, but some made me believe that they thought I was amazing, like Kira had. Sometimes I could pretend they were my girlfriend or boyfriend and that I had a future. They told me I was beautiful.

Twenty-seven. I knew my death was coming. Often, I couldn't wake up to my usual alarm, and if I did, fatigue dragged me to bed an hour later. I learned to pray at the end, though I didn't know who or what I prayed to, or what I prayed for. *Make it okay*, I said sometimes, vaguely, before sleep took me away. I woke at strange times for only a few minutes together, some days sleeping more than thirty hours straight. I woke up to my parents crying at my bedside more than once, like waking up at my own funeral. *Maybe a prince will wake me in a hundred years*, I said to my mom once, but she only cried, and I hugged her.

Against the odds, I did reach my twenty-eighth birthday. I had a few bites of the cake my parents delivered with teary smiles, and then asked them for space. In the days afterward, I inhaled caffeine—something I had learned as a teenager would make things better for a few hours, and then so much worse afterward that it wasn't worth it—and began to write. I wrote my story, with that old scraggly cat curled up at my side. It seemed important that my story be there for someone, though it was more full of questions than answers—Should I have done something differently? Was this the best life I could have lived?

Did it matter, now?

Maybe, I wrote it for Kira, though I knew she was engaged, knew that her life had kept going like a shooting star flying past into another world. Maybe, I wrote it for those old dreams that I traced like scars, dreams of living with her, dreams of a career, of staying on the same path as those old, never-quite-forgotten friends.

Maybe, I wrote it for the lost.

LISA LOW
DOING A GOOD JOB AT SIXTY

Last night the snow came down in a fury.
A sky-wide flurry of white winged beauty.
This morning standing knee-high in it,
I dreaded the thought of having to thin it.
I had to drive myself to continue: to
bend and shove, and bend and shove, the
curved steel forward, to gather and throw
the heavy snow over tired shoulder
and elbow. But as the minutes grew to
hours, and snow removed became a path
to follow, the work became lighter, the
load less heavy; then, instead of hurrying
to finish, I slowed, wanting to clean the
edge of the well and square the dark curb
neatly. Easy it is to lie on the ground and
gaze enraptured at the sun. Necessity is
harder. It drives you through resistance:
the earth's; your own, until the path is clear.
Sweet the waters of relaxation. Far more
thrilling: the joy of a job well done.

Low

IOWA HEAT

On my own in a strange state with a flat
tire and no gas. A man in boots steps from
the strip to help. He crouches low using his
thighs for a shelf and rubs his jaw to think.
He jacks up the car from the rear; reaches
his hand between the flanks; flicks the bolts
in quick, short circles off. When the rim
leaps free, without a word of nay, he
brushes up against me.   I tell him I teach;
read; write poetry. He says he shoots
rabbit, deer, the Japanese; buys American;
runs a farm. The afternoon lingers, like a
finger on a rim. On it our bodies buzz: legs
tense; haunches high; needle points raised.

Low

VINCENT J TOMEO
PHYSICS AND MAMA

Sitting at the dining room table a cloud on my face, sad, worried. How will I ever pass my physics examination, I thought to myself. Mama asked, "What's wrong?" "Mama! I am going to fail physics. I simply don't understand either the theories or the concepts. The professor is trying to transfer in terms of physics, I can't articulate the knowledge I did not gain. What do I do?"

We, Mama and I, brainstormed.
"Did you seek out tutoring? Ask the professor for clarification, help, and assistance." "Mama, he never seems to have time for me; when my schedule is free, he is teaching. When he is free, I am in class or working. What do I do?"
"Go to the library," Mama said. "And what do I do there, when I don't understand what I am reading?" "Start from the beginning," Mama said.
"What do you mean, Mama?"
"Refer to the most elementary physics books for children, and work

your way up. See if this will help to clarify the subject matter."

So, the next day, off I went to the library. This became a habit, and I spent a great deal of my spare time in the library. I studied the basic fundamentals of physics for children, probably a third-grade level, with illustrations. Every day I would survey, examine, and inspect the subject repeatedly. I began to work my way up through the grade levels. The simple figures, diagrams, formulas, and language helped me to grasp the subject matter, although I thought this was not university material, nevertheless I kept at it.

Finally, it was the examination day. I was nervous. I took the exam and culled from my mind the elementary readings I had read, my newly gained information, and even included some simple illustrations, formulas, and theories, too, which I learned from the first primary education books. That week I worried about how I did on my test.

One week later, I received my examination in physics from my professor with the following comments: "love your simplicity of style, your economy of language, your illustrations prove you have a real understanding of physics. You are on the mark. Kudos!" I received an A grade. Thank you, mama!

THOMAS A WEST, JR
TWINS

When I'm beside myself
my other half is watching,
often as not sadly shaking
his head as if to say no,
    that's not right. He is my
conscience, yet con-science
is against truth, just as con-
cave negates spelunking.

(cont)

And just why does my brain
resemble a miniature cave
where I go exploring who I am,
how I came to be here in this
Now. If there are two of me,
who is observing when I dream?
   The one beside me nudges:
          write this down or you'll
               forget it.

Where, other than up here, is a
cave that's barely lit by
phosphorescent ideas which cling
like bats to walls, ready to fly
at night, eyeless, all the way to
my den,   write this down, now.

The cave is mine inside myself,
and I'm just whistling in the dark.

West

CLARE COOPER MARCUS
DEAD PHEASANTS

This time I saw them and remembered

"Three pounds fifty a brace"
the sign said above the box of
dead pheasants
eyes clouded milky cumulus
feathers berry-red and green
like winter ivy fading to
angry bruising of betrayal

(cont)

I remember you strutting like
jeweled princes in the sunlit fields
of childhood
I remember proud tails
regal collars
raucous cries when danger
lurked

I remember wallowing in the cooling
waters of a brook we thought of as
 the Nile
climbing a beech tree in a wind
that tempest-tossed our bodies
till we felt sick with ecstasy

Mornings full of horses' hoofs
on cobbles
swallows in black arrow
squadrons diving low over piles of
steaming dung
evenings full of dark-bodied planes
returning from missions dropping
death

The pheasants lie close
as lovers
breast upon breast
as in the aching scar of Babi Yar
where bodies pressed
 bone upon bone
in the unfamiliar intimacy of
death

Marcus

JULIE OWSIK ACKERMAN
ACROSS THE BORDER

Saturday afternoon, I stood in the bedroom I shared with Dulce, my shy, thirteen-year-old host sister. A short towel wrapped me from armpits to thighs, my hair dripped down my shoulders and back, and leather *chanclas* protected my feet from any scorpions that lurked. Surveying my limited outfit choices, I sighed. Mexican women dressed more formally than American college students in general, but what does one wear for a walk in the countryside with Miguel?

I settled on a black, cotton skirt and tank top, with my sturdy walking sandals, then peeked out the upstairs window and saw Miguel sitting outside already, a few minutes early. I let myself stare, taking in his neatly-ironed khaki pants, his long-sleeve white shirt casually rolled at the wrists, and gold, chain-link bracelet glinting in the sun, beautiful on his dark skin. He exuded confidence, self-possession. I smoothed my skirt down over my hips, gave my hair a final scrunch, and took a deep breath before walking downstairs and opening the gate, which squawked my arrival. He stood and turned toward me, smiling.

"*Buenas tardes*," he said.

"*Buenas tardes*," I responded, feeling shy, nervous.

He hesitated, then pointed uphill. "We'll have to walk this way a bit to reach the bridge across the stream."

I loved that he slowed down his Spanish enough so I could understand him. "Okay."

We walked up to the fork in the road and took another branch of the *calle* down toward the bottom of the ravine where we crossed a small, cement bridge over the stream. On our left sat a house with a yard containing a giant sow nursing piglets, a donkey, a bunch of chickens and a rooster.

"Huh. There's the bastard who wakes me up every morning," I said, giving the rooster my dirtiest look. Miguel's laugh thrilled me because I made him laugh in Spanish.

"You're not used to roosters, I guess," he said.

"No. And I thought they only sang one time, at dawn. But no, he crows every five minutes starting at four a.m."

"I guess they do. I don't even hear them. City girl, huh?"

"Suburban."

"No pigs there either?"

"*Tampoco*."

I loved how easy it was to talk to him, though I wondered for a moment why he had learned to simplify his Spanish—for another *güera*? If you're a desirable, twenty-year-old guy, and ten American girls moved into your neighborhood each year, surely you have dated a few. *It doesn't matter, Laura.*

"Is it crowded like here where you're from?" he asked.

I looked around, noticing that as we ascended the other side of the ravine, we had left civilization behind. Surrounding us, long grass and wildflowers swished and swayed, and small, white butterflies floated over undulating hills.

"This doesn't look very crowded."

"I meant the *colonia*, funny girl."

I savored the word "funny." "My town is very close to Filadelfia, and the whole area around the city is pretty crowded. There's no open space like this, except in parks."

"*Qué lastima.*"

Was it a shame? I'd never thought about it. It just was. "Nobody lives over here?" I asked.

"A few people do." He paused, then reached out his hand to swipe a leaf. "Look." He opened his hand, revealing a grasshopper before letting it go again, then indicated I should walk in front of him on the narrow path. "Cuernavaca basically ends with our neighborhood, which was only built within the last twenty years. Before, this was all countryside."

I glanced back at him. "Do you remember before the street was built?"

"*Sí.* I helped build it."

I pictured tiny Miguel, carrying a bucket of water to mix with cement and smiled at the thought.

"What?" he asked.

"I'm imagining you as a kid."

"Yeah? What do I look like?"

I turned to face him, squinted, considering. "Basically the same, only smaller."

He grinned. "That's about right. And you? Like this but smaller?"

I flashed on childhood photos and winced. "No. I had short hair, more freckles—pretty ugly."

"*Mentirosa.*"

I smiled at his disbelief. "It's true. My brother still calls me Dennis the Menace. That's an insult," I added, in case he didn't know who that was.

"Brothers are mean. I'm sure you were always beautiful."

"Then why are you laughing?" We were both laughing, and again I noticed the ease of our conversation.

"Here, this way," he said, climbing onto a big rock, putting out his hand and pulling me up next to him, the feel of his skin on mine sending warmth up my arm, jump-starting my heart. If he was similarly distracted, he didn't show it. Instead, he pointed toward the horizon at two large mountains, one with a snow-capped peak. "See over there? That's Popocatepetl and Iztaccíhuatl," he said.

"What?"

He repeated the impossible names. As if Spanish wasn't hard enough, many things in Mexico had names in indigenous languages.

"You haven't heard their story?"

I shook my head. "Tell me."

We sat down on the rock, his thigh touching mine through our clothes, my skin tingling accordingly. His eyes got a little dreamy and far away.

"*Bueno*, the Emperor and Empress of the Nahuatls had only one child, late in life. They named her Iztaccíhuatl, which means 'white woman.'"

"A *güera*?"

He turned to me and smiled. "*Sí*, like you.

"Iztaccíhuatl, Izta, was a beautiful princess. Her parents wanted her to marry well and picked out many suitors, but she rejected them all because she wanted to marry for love. One day, she was walking in the hills, not far from here, and met a handsome warrior named Popoca. When their eyes met, something powerful happened between them—they both felt it, even though it was hard to explain. Love at first sight. Luckily, he was exactly the kind of husband her parents would have wanted for her, but unluckily, he was from a different tribe."

He paused and studied my face. "Are you understanding me?"

I nodded. The words I understood. If there were similarities between what he was describing and what I felt about us, I refused to entertain them.

"So Popoca asked the Emperor for his daughter's hand in marriage, but the Emperor said he would only allow it if Popoca's people fought with the Nahautls against their enemy. He assumed that either they wouldn't fight, or if they did, that Popoca wouldn't survive. But such was his love that Popoca convinced his tribe to fight with the Nahautls, and after a long and bloody battle, they emerged victorious."

I was drawn into his story, but not enough to forget about his leg touching mine, or the warm boulder under our thighs, or the sunshine on my face.

"So did they live happily ever after?"

He looked at me, then back at the mountains. "No. That was not their fate. Popoca had enemies among his tribe, warriors who were jealous of his courage and success. One of them secretly sent word back to the Emperor that Popoca had been killed in the battle. When Izta heard the news, she fell into a deep depression and died of a broken heart, unable to live without her one true love."

I sucked in a breath, shaken. Franklin appeared before my eyes, lying on his living room floor, eyes open, unresponsive, victim of a physically broken heart.

"Weeks later, when Popoca returned in triumph to claim his bride, he found the Nahuatls preparing her funeral. Devastated, he took her body up into the mountains, laid her down, knelt to watch over her and died of grief. The gods, who saw the exceptional love of Popoca and Izta, took pity on them, and turned them into mountains so they could remain together for all time."

There I am, kneeling over Franklin. I've come back from the accident, ready to do more battle, and he has died. He's fucking died.

I put my hands over my face, trying to erase this image, substitute the legendary lovers, or Miguel and me.

"Are you okay?" he asked.

"It's real, right? That's how things turn out. Popoca did everything he was supposed to, and he still lost her." I hopped off the boulder and began pacing. "But why couldn't he grieve, and heal? Why did he have to die with her?"

Miguel slid down the rock and stepped next to me. "I like the idea that for some of us, there is only one right person who is meant to be their love. I guess for Popoca, he knew there could never be anyone else."

He pointed out the curves in the one mountain. "Do you see how she looks like a sleeping woman? Her head, her chest, her knees? And there's Popo, kneeling beside her. Every once in a while, he sends smoke up to let us know that he's still watching over her."

I became suddenly aware of his body, so close to mine. I looked down, heat rushing to my face.

He leaned toward me and traced a finger down my cheek. "I love the roses on your face."

I covered my cheeks with my hands. "I hate them."

"*Ay, qué lastima,*" he said, gently removing my hands, "because they're beautiful." He lightly brushed my still-warm cheeks, then leaned closer and kissed me, first gently, then with growing urgency, his hands roving over my back, pulling me closer.

Yes, lips on my neck. Yes, hands under my shirt. He pressed against me, hard between my legs, our breath fast and shallow. Oh God. The straps of my tank top and bra, down, shoulder bare. Yes. Make me forget everything. Then a pause. His fingers lightly traced the puckered skin of my scar.

I jerked back, pulling my straps up and hugging my arms over my chest.

"I'm sorry," he said. "Are you…okay?"

I turned away, nodding.

His hand on my arm made me flinch.

"Laura, can you look at me?"

He wasn't the first person to see my scars. So why did it feel like he was? I turned slowly, looking at his chest. He tucked a hair behind my ear.

"Do they hurt?" he asked.

I looked up at his face, his green eyes full of concern.

"Not in the way you might think."

I wanted to sprint, away from his gaze that studied me. It was too much. I looked toward the mountains. Did Izta die of a broken heart or from fear? Is it the same thing?

"I can go as slow as you need to," he said.

"Okay."

He didn't ask. That is my only explanation for hearing the truth fall out of my mouth.

"I was hit by a car."

He swiveled his head.

"That's why I have the scars. I was out for a jog, training, and a woman blew a stop sign and ran right into me. I didn't even see her coming."

"*Dios.*" He took my hand. "When was that?"

"Two years ago." I extracted my hand, turned toward home.

"So, that's why you stopped playing tennis?"

No. I had come back from the accident, and could have been even stronger, but Franklin's death changed everything. I couldn't fight without my coach. I couldn't even pick up a racket. But I didn't say any of that to Miguel. Too many people had made it worse with their well-meaning attempts to comfort: you're young, you can find another coach; he's in a better place; or, my favorite, he would want you to keep playing. As if they fucking knew anything.

Miguel kept a respectful distance. "I'm sorry you went through that."

"Shit happens, right? I guess everyone learns at some point that bad things can come out of nowhere and change your life forever."

Miguel nodded, and we started to walk back toward the *colonia*. "Good things can come out of nowhere too," he said eventually. "They can show up in your neighborhood, from another country, to name a random example."

I turned to see him smiling, bringing me back to the present, back to this sunny day where this god of a man reached for my hand, and kissed it. The sun caressed the top of my head, and the grass swayed against my legs.

Maybe we weren't Izta and Popo. Maybe their story didn't fit any of my stories. Maybe Franklin had died, taking my tennis dreams with him, but maybe new dreams were possible. Maybe I had come to Mexico to find out what they were.

I plucked a wildflower and inhaled. "Maybe you're right."

The warrior-lover-volcanoes kept watch over us as we made our way down the steep hill, past the rooster, sow and piglets, over the bridge and back into the unlikely neighborhood that stretched down the side of a ravine, on the outskirts of the City of Eternal Spring.

MARC KAMINSKY
IN THE SOUND OF SHATTERING GLASS

In the sound of shattering
glass, muteness
returns, emptiness

You have nothing
to fall back on
but language, but
nothing comes
to you who are known
to be so quick
to give the moment
its life back
in words. You turn off

(cont)

the TV and stare
at the window, at the dust
motes in the dirty
light at the window.

As a boy, after shattering
times, you sat
in the silence, repeating
a word—it didn't matter what
word—speeding through it countless times until
it was mere sound, sheer
nonsense. Astounded
at how fragile words are,
how easily you drove the meaning out
of them. Now the talking
heads do the same, repeating
the same phrases, turning
every disaster to drivel.

In the hour of shattered
glass, minutes
are thickly woven nets dragged
along the bottom
of violent seas,
scooping up days, eras, eternities.

The black plume overhead
on 9/11 dropped
white ash
on your house and garden
for seven weeks,
you breathed in the dead
until your legs couldn't bear
your lungs any longer,

you tried coughing
out the killing
air and couldn't stop
coughing

(cont)

until you keeled over, inert,
your wife thought you had died.

In the silence after the shattering
blast, you go on
waiting for the sound of shattering glass.

You think: waiting for the other
shoe to drop.

You think you think in language,
but now, as words return,
you see that
the language thinks you.

You're waiting
for the other shoe
to drop, as if
proverbial speech had some relief
to offer, but it isn't a shoe,

the wired
pressure cooker in the middle
of 23rd Street is probably a bomb,
the shock-
waves from the armed pot
that exploded a block away
go on and on, destroying
space, time, language,
thought, leaving you
orphaned in an orphaning
time, watching white ash float before
your eyes, suspended
between Kristallnacht and the towers
that never stopped
falling

(cont)

If you were to climb
up to your roof
or drive across the Brooklyn Bridge,
you'd see the New York skyline
lying open to the sky,
rocking back and forth in the wind.

Kaminsky

THE GIFT OF A STORY
to my mother Mintzie

1 Face to Face with You

In your blank stare, Mother, I see you
trying to look pensive until
confusion passes and you remember
where you've met me before.
Here at this kitchen table,

I did my duty by you, putting up
with long delays when signal systems failed
or a line was out for track repair,
changing trains three or more times,
at least an hour and a half each way
between my stop in Brooklyn

and your end of the Bronx. I'd show up
and space out when you became weird,
teasing an insidious attack out of a benign
remark or a gift of food, an Old World appetizer
or dessert, stuffed derma or rugelakh.
You believed that I was accusing you
of failing to a provide a seven-course dinner, like
your Bessarabian mother used to cook for us.

Why did I keep coming back, determined
to make friends with you before
the time we were given came to an end?
And yet I knew:

(cont)

I wanted to bring home to you
an obscure and invincible gratitude
for the gift of life that made your face
the one I woke up to, in the beginning?

Even when you destroyed my good
will and I felt less
than kind toward you, I worked
hard to remain unprovoked, innocuous,
as you stared at the chair
which contained me as if I weren't there.

I went blank to avoid knowing
what I felt: horror
that you were annihilating me through
the eyes of what looked like your death
mask, your face screaming
through your frozenness, a woman by Ensor.

Now I see you trying to hide
your struggle to preserve what remains
of your dignity. You are aware
that Alzheimer's is erasing letters
from street signs, stealing your keys,
turning you into a shut-in.

Earlier today, you learned once
again that you and Mintzie are one
and the same person, then
that person got lost in a wilderness
of forgetting where the pathways
between your name
and your tongue have been eroded.

Inside your skull, stringy black
tangles and clumpy brown plaques
are microscopically eating away all
that connects you to yourself
and the world. But I see you, Mother:

(cont)

behind your blank stare, you are
still at work, hoping
to find a way around the debris
floating through your brain, and come back
into the room with my name.

2 Through the Doorway

After a lifetime in which you felt me taking
bites out of you, and I felt the same,
the kitchen where we devoured each other
has become a quiet place: here

I hold your bony hand with its trembling
fingers and wormlike veins crawling
along your skin, and I tell you
the story of how you were good for me.

On the morning after the election of 1952,
you didn't burst into the room to wake us.
An alarm went off in me, I jumped
out of bed, rushed to the kitchen, found you

in front of the refrigerator, frozen,
as if you'd opened the door and forgotten
what you came for. I asked, What's wrong,
Ma? You snapped out of your reverie

and said, It's Eisenhower, he won,
your voice filled with sorrow and concern
that included me. I didn't know until now
it was an event in my life.

Years later, although it seemed to have
occurred the next day, I didn't see you
hurrying from stove to closet to table
the way you usually did at dawn.

(cont)

You had your back to me, in its slight
heaves I heard the soundless tears
you were crying. Sensing me

behind you, watching from the doorway,
you turned and said, Camus is dead
Killed in a car accident last night.
Your grief for your loss and the world's
had a place in it for me. Your devastation

was the most personal thing you'd ever
disclosed to me. I wanted to comfort
you and knew I couldn't. And then
somewhere between Eisenhower's election

and Camus' death, I stopped in the kitchen
doorway to say good-bye to you
before my first date ever. I was
wearing a flamboyant red corduroy coat

and sporting a high pompadour.
You smiled and said, You look nice.
I'd forgotten that we ever had
a perfectly ordinary mother-son exchange.

It's enough to make me believe
that when you insisted
in the midst of one of our raging
fights that you had always

loved me passionately, always
been proud of me, it wasn't
a lie. I imagine there were
innumerable unremembered quiet times

when I folded myself up
in your lap; I must have brought you
happiness early on, moments that left
spores of tenderness and sanity in me.

(cont)

Here in this quietude, I relive finding
intimacy with you in the public
world that passed through your kitchen;
your caring for the world helped

form me as a listener, who began
hearing the pre-history of the women's
movement hidden in your rages
against the endless mess in the house.
There are moments in our lives
that hate cannot find
and that wait for us
to stumble across them again.

Such moments, if rightly placed,
are the doorway where we
cross over to the loving kindness
we need to renovate our days.

As I remember our good times,
you drift into a light sleep,
disengage your hand from mine,
then wake up, startled. Where's Mama...

no, wait...where's my sugar bowl...oh,
you must be my son Marc...very nice...
such a nice visit...good-bye...
let's do this again sometime.

Kaminsky

IN HIDING

After my father sang me
lullabies of the Holocaust,
I lay in the dark of my waking
dream, singing a little

(cont)

Yiddish song I made up;
it kept me company
in the coffin my narrow bed
turned into. *Aleyn*

vi a shteyn. Alone
like a stone. Yet I went on
looking for my father's eyes.
And lo! they rose

over the edge of the plain
pine box that held
my body. He gazed down
at me, grief-stricken at last.

He'd been so busy
caring for the dead,
he'd missed
his chance with me in this life,

and there was small likelihood
he would sit at a bench
studying Torah with me
in the next. Ghostlike, we

passed each other in the hallways
of that Bronx apartment
seventeen years before
I removed the apparition

of myself from their midst.
How many times have I
told this story? Coffin, Yiddish,
ghosts--what happened

to me didn't happen
to me, I wasn't there, I
wasn't the one who suffered.
The strangest part of all

(cont)

is that even then I knew
joy, my brush loaded
with yellow, painting a patch
of sunlight on a wall.

Moments when I forgot
where I was flared into
life with a faith that flit
past words, the words

spoken in that house
died in mid-air between
the tongue that spoke them
and the ears that mangled them.

In the bits of pleroma I painted,
I stored for later use
my Marrano matzah and wine.
I hid it all so well, even I

didn't know the secret
hope that visited me as I thrust
my loaded brush against the supple canvas:
there has to be something better than this.

Kaminsky

AN ORDINARY LIFE
to my sister Riva

Long ago, in another century, I lived
in the tale my father told me.
First-born, Jewish, male, inheritor
of his blood: he showed me
our future in his praise
of the brooding faces I painted.
My art would prove the genius
he carried in his genes was real.

(cont)

At six I set to work, a zealot
in my father's cause, and mine.
By seven, Rembrandt was my ideal—
no, I can't, I've repeated this tale
countless times, it no
longer involves me, its recital
ties me to the past,
deadens me to myself, unless

the old hunger for greatness
rises up, turns me against
the life I've patched together,
and I burn for my sweet father
to sing me to sleep, until
by retelling my own story backward
and forward, I break away from
my rapacious father's embrace again.

I was once the genius
of the household, crowned prodigy and prince
of the old kingdom of my father's tale.
My special place at his table was underwritten
by the biblical law of primogeniture.

Since then, that glorious self returns
at an uncertain hour
and holds me in contempt, itemizing
the laurels I've failed to win, charging
me with envy of my friends' achievements.

Oh, I paid for my ill-will, my self-
absorption, my obliviousness of my brother
and sister masked craving I couldn't
keep down. I cracked up three
or four times in my twenties, worked hard

(cont)

to abdicate my throne and participate
in the common life, with its mutual projects
and feast days, its inspired stumblings
and accidental splendors, but then
I crash into the monumental failure

of seeking glory as a self-cure
for shame, and sink into my former
intimacy with hollowness. I
reduce the manyness of self that drifts
through my days into a battle royal

between two antagonists—one great,
the other ordinary—losing the openness
to change I attained by becoming sick
and tired of not wanting to be
what I am until I go through being

divided again and come out of it
as if I were just one person, the one
who's grateful for the ongoing hum
of love in my life and takes pleasure
in putting my limited gifts to use.

Kaminsky

MICHAEL J SHEPLEY
WHAT SHE SAID

"She says only the ugly kids have to be rats."

Rats...OK. The school "ballet." It is Xmas tide. So, of course, the Nutcracker gets released from its yearly solitary confinement again. More's the pity, as his dear old mom was wont to say. Bit of the auld turf surviving through three gens on. It's in the blood, as she also had liked to say. He trended more towards "nurture," himself. Probably that generational pendulum reaction. In theory.

"Who?"

"Who who?"

"Who her?" he realized immediately that that sounded absolutely ridiculous while being badly insufficient. "What girl is harassing you with that sorta mishmosh?"

He was vaguely aware his daughter had inherited her own mother's nails-on-chalkboard petulant whiney tone. A tone he had somehow missed until about the first year anniversary, actually.

"Eee-liz-ah-BETH!"

Ah. Sure. The little blond thing with the cupie face. Looks like an angel, but she is the devil. Uh-huh.

"Well, Lilly-Bee is trying to sell you shoeshine as applebutter, babydoll. You look fine..." oooops, too light on the honey that... "you look great. And she's just jealous."

"Of what?"

Boy, had he painted that proverbial corner bit. Hmmm— "Because...you have one of the best parts! King of the mice!"

"It's King Rat, Daddy!"

He shot her a look. But she could not know about the book. Maybe she had watched the flick on the tube one time...Nah! Irony...way beyond her still tender years.

"They're just mice, honey."

"Dirty old rats!" Period. Point.

I am not playing the word volley game, he thought.

"Whatever. It's only pretend. Costume. For a show. And you get a real neat costume. Does she?"

He saw thought fill her little round face. Tiny brown brows furrowed over her shining black eyes. Then, slow and long she said—

"Nooooo."

"And you have a crown, too."

That should have been game and set. But noooo.

"She gets to be the Princess!"

Not a princess. But why get long-winded with the 'she's just a girl at a family party' bit? How long would all that take to explain...This Lilly chick was clearly a narcissistic little B....

But to parry his daughter's point—

"Does she get to sword fight?"

"No." Short and sweet.

Good. Now game, set. Not quite match, however....

They marched on into a brisk wind, not terrible, but winter. Going a tad uphill, not steep, but a city slope. Just three and a half or so blocks. Not much choice, he thought, watching her little engine that could breaths puffing over her shoulder behind them.

Like you'd call a cab?

Drop a Lincoln each way. Take the cabbie's abuse, then hand him a couple paper Washingtons for a tip?

Hey, back in the day, right around her age too, out in practically farm country, he had trudged two miles through a blizzard in his face the whole way to school, then trudged back the two miles to home with the same blizzard in his face. And uphill both times, to boot.

He had told her that tale a number of times.

In fact the last time had been as he fought to get her little snap boots on wiggly feet just before this cool hike.

She had yet to disparage it.

He was waiting for that day, when she called him on what that was.

A little test.

But, for now....

"Look at those little birds," she virtually squealed.

She was pointing to the foot of a city tree locked in its small square of concrete surrounded dirt. Three tiny, about the size of an adult thumb, yellow-breasted birds were flitting and hopping. Like playing tag.

Squabbling, probably. Nature of the beasties.

"Why are they doing THAT?"

"Oh...playing, maybe."

"Why would they play?"

"Dunno...it's in their genes, I guess."

That kept her quiet as they walked past.

And that quiet scared him. It could bring no good.

"Ummm...", he started, slow, "you know what genes are? Not like pants...."

"Dad-EEE. I'm not dumb. DNA."

And why in the world would she have learned that, already. Things in kids' world were getting accelerated in a crazy way. Not that anyone cared what he had to say about it.

He would not try to explain the dif between dumb, and IQ impaired.

Again.

That would be too stupid.

Dumb, even.

He was just glad Lilly-butt had finally left the proverbial building.

Except then his daughter asked—

"Are they really going to chop off my head?"

Hell NO! Who?

"And just what are you talking about, little lady?"

"The soldiers. And the Prince."

"Ummm...what Prince?"

"In our dance. Eee-liz...."

Ah, that pint-sized little witch was back again, invisibly, but definitely.

"No. Definitely not. The only head that comes off is the Nutcracker's, remember. And only early, when he is a toy."

And those little dark eyes looked up in serious doubt askance—

"Are you sure?"

Like father no longer could know best. Surprise.

But before he said anything he thought on things a second longer. Hey, once physics had been all certain, billiard balls and plain geometric lines. Now it was all a cloud in flux full of probability waves collapsing here and there practically willynilly. In a universe like that who could say he was absolutely sure of anything?

Maybe someone had taken liberties.

Perhaps the teacher/director had some very Grimm issues.

Really, who knew...until that psi wave collapsed too.

"I don't think so."

Best he could do. Didn't sound convincing.

"But she says....."

She's a flippin' idjut—another of Mom's wise phrases—he wanted to yell it out.

But he stifled the urge, and his little girl finished the sentence-

"...that they cut my head...."

"The King of the Mice's head."

"The Rat King's...."

"Let's just split the difference—Rodent Monarch's...."

She shrugged. A push. Knock knock.

"...and drag my body...."

Ah, well....

"...to burn it up in a ditch."

"No. Nope. No heads get cut off like that. Nobody gets burned up. Do you think they'd let someone start a fire in your school? The...rodents...carry the dead king away in honor."

This was becoming a bloody Greek tragedy. Or some sort of Shakespeare slagfest on the half shell.

"Are you sure?"

Man! Again!

"Every time I've seen it that's what happens."

"How many times have you seen it?"

Over a thousand!

"Oh...maybe 10...12 times. It never changes. Trust me."

Unless some psycho is channeling Titus Andronicus.

She was stuck turning his assurance over in her mind.

"Ah, look! There's the store."

At freaking last.

"You said I could get strudel."

"Yep."

"What are you getting?"

"Supper, you know that."

"But what?"

He started to say, but balked. There was a pitfall lurking in the answer somewheres. Had to be.

After a couple more steps he started off slow, and careful-

"A loaf of nice Italian bread."

"Uh-huh."

"A bottle of red vino."

"Yeh."

Ah...there it was—the soup! That was the big problemo!

"And a liter container of their soup."

"What kind."

What to say. Not tortellini. For some reason she hated tortellini.

Ah—

"Italian wonton."

She eyed him—

"Really?"

"Yeh. Marco Polo brought the recipe back from China himself. That's where he discovered pasta you know."

She looked away and groused—

"I heard mommy say turtle-beany."

"No. Daddy wanted something else. Something better. So that's what we'll get."

She became way too quiet again as he swung open the old-style bell-ring door and a heaven of warm, sweet and savory aroma put its tractor beam on his now hungry nose, pulling. Pulling him inside.

She said, "I don't ever want to eat a turtle."

"Neither do I", he said back quick, and wondered how to sell the wonton thing...AH YES! Put the little bottle of soy sauce on the table, she loved the stuff. That'd do it.

Mom had better go along....

His hand was yanked hard, as if it were holding onto a chain in a rowboat where someone had thrown over the anchor.

He glanced down. She was stopped dead on the threshold, looking a little sad, like Shirley Temple without the fake pout, looking back all the way up at him, way way up there in the air.

"Am I ugly?"

"Honey," he said, a hard chest ache grabbing his air, "You are so beautiful."

She stared at him a handful more of small heartbeats, then... "Really?"

MAUREEN GERAGHTY
NARCISSUS

At Christmas, I bought the $4.99 box of bulbs,
pulled the dusty orbs from plastic package
and stuck them, stem side up in the powdered dirt.
I put the pot near a heater vent, kept the soil moist
as the green shoots grew tall, pods formed on top
and through their thin veil, flower buds visible—
miniature globes of white waiting, waiting
for flawless chemistry of light and time
to effortlessly exact one wing of Narcissus
into the world announcing
its fresh white,
its undeniable presence.
The morning I woke, and was stopped
by this announcement of flower,
I couldn't help but marvel
the way things that begin
in dirt, in dark,

(cont)

in small gestures of tenderness
can sometimes
startle a day with
exquisite revolution.

Geraghty

RAIN

Some days clouds can no longer carry their gray,
surrender the heavy,
spilling the sky on a planet so thirsty,
it puddles with Hope.

Geraghty

PAUL BOWMAN
DAD

The young man parked his car near the barn, his usual parking space, and walked to the trees that bordered the first pasture, a short distance away. He stood under branches and leaves that filtered the light of the moon. A slight wind tickled the green-black leaves. He heard a rustle. The young man bowed his head and looked at the ground. He put his hands in his pockets.

I've been a bitch she had said with the smallest smile. Not an apology. A brag.

It was almost ten p.m. and he was home already. He looked up and touched a leaf. He wished he could go to bed and fall asleep instantly. Without a thought.

He walked to the house. An old man stood on the back porch and watched his approach.

"What's wrong?"

There was concern in the man's face, voice, and posture. He stared, ready to receive the news of an accident or disaster. His thin, white hair, unkempt at all times, silvery in the moonlight, reminded the son of a goat's hair. He wore pajama bottoms and slippers. No top. His belly was round, soft. His chest was smaller and hairy. The strong jaw was covered with the stubble of two, three day's growth of whiskers. The man waited.

"You ok?"

"Yes," said David.

"I saw you drive in. You didn't come to the house."

David did not reply.

"You take a leak?"

"No."

The son imagined what his father must be thinking. *So what were you doing? Talking to the trees?*

"You going to bed?"

"Eventually!"

"What are you getting mad about??"

"Nothing."

The old father, turned, and went to his bed in the house. His son watched him without any feeling of compassion or disgust. He regretted that he hadn't stopped by a liquor store on the way home. He needed to drink away his disappointment.

***

Christmas Eve and a full house. Brother Steve, his wife Darlene, and their two boys. His sister Vinnie, her husband, Bob, and their two boys. Mom. Dad. And him. He sat in the corner of the living room, watching the play of the four boys.

"Uncle David!" yelled one as he raced by.

The other adults stood and sat in the kitchen and talked. David put the JOBS NOW! WEEKLY paper on the floor. Nothing in there to apply for. What did he expect? Nobody hired on Christmas Eve. Nobody had been hiring for months. Seven months. David looked at the Christmas tree and hated its glittering gaudiness. Four of the gifts under the tree were from him to his nephews. He had sold his plasma twice a week for two months to pay for them. He got thirty dollars the first visit, Tuesday, and thirty five the second donation, usually Thursday, sometimes Friday. It had felt strange at first being in the plasma center with the derelicts, winos, and losers. He got used to them. He brought along a book to read while he waited for the needle stick. Right arm, Tuesdays; left arm, Thursdays.

"Lately I've been in close to fifty hours a week," said Steve in the kitchen.

"Seems like I'm doing about the same," said Bob. "Usually spring is our busy season, but it's been hectic lately. People are buying carpet like crazy."

David put his hands together as if he were praying. His forefingers were pressed against his lips. He knew the upcoming night and the following day would be a bad time for him, but he could wait it out. Just say nothing. On December 26 everything would be the same again.

"David?" said his mother from the kitchen. "We're all having eggnog. Do you want some eggnog?"

No, he did not.

***

They met in the inner office. The interviewer placed the resume on his desk and studied it.

"You have several gaps in your employment history. Why is that?"

David hesitated. "It just turned out that way. I didn't want it to."

The interviewer watched him and repeated his words. "Turned out that way."

David stared at the phone on the desk. He wanted to look through the window just to avoid the man's critical eyes, but that would have been too obvious.

"Three of the places I worked at went out of business. The last job was temporary job to begin with. You can't always find something new right away."

"I see you do not have restaurant experience. Why don't you walk into one of our locations and just watch and observe. To see what goes on. It's a fast-paced environment."

"I've been to fast-food restaurants before."

"We'll be making our decision in a week."

Ok. You don't like me. I get it.

***

He heard a noise. A chair moving against the vinyl floor. Footsteps. An intruder was in the house. In the kitchen. David forced himself to sit up. The bed groaned. He listened. The house and the intruder were silent. David slipped off the creaking bed and stood. He walked toward the kitchen.

His naked father stood before the sliding glass patio door. He was a figure both familiar and unfamiliar, intimate and strange. He looked through the glass at the irregular line of trees at the end of the pasture. His rapt gaze was focused on something distant. Perhaps a memory.

His father was shorter than he had remembered. The white hair wild again. The upper back slumped over. The man's skin sagged at places: the upper arms, once muscular, the chest, the neck. His legs had thinned. His penis was limp, wrinkled. David thought it strange to know that it had once created him. The long scrotum had been stretched by time and gravity.

"Dad?"

His father did not hear him. He continued to look through the glass and savor that something that was across the night grass and into the trees. What was it?

"Go to bed, Dad."

David touched his father's forearm to lead him to his bedroom. The man's face turned and David was given a glimpse of the man's private terror. The blue eyes were sharp, intense.

***

The walk down the wide corridor required a tightening of the breath and a resolute pace. Faces peered at him from bodies in wheelchairs. A woman cried, "Help me. Help me. Oh, please help me." The stench of urine emanated from one room. He heard a bell repeat a *ding ding ding ding ding ding*. One resident, a thin, small man, his hands folded in his lap, sat in his wheelchair, and gave him a look of deep-seated hate. A tiny woman stopped him in the corridor. She wore a sweater over her dress and carried a child's purse.

"What time does the bus come? The bus. I'm going to Florida to see my boy. What time does the bus come?"

David looked down to avoid her gaze and saw the worn slippers on her feet. He said *excuse me* and walked around her.

"What time does the bus come?"

David entered Room 127. His father was asleep in a chair. The head hung downward and appeared to be too large and heavy for his neck.

David came every day. He was the only who did. Everyone else had jobs. His visits were maintenance sessions. His father slept more and talked less. When he did speak it was sullen words or nonsense syllables. David walked over and touched his father's shoulder. The man woke.

"Morning, Dad. It's me. David."

He received a wary look.

David began his routine. He removed the false teeth and took them to the sink to brush them. He washed his father's face and shaved him. He held the hair brush under the hot water of the water faucet and brought the brush to the man's head. He combed his hair.

"There. You look five years younger."

An aide rolled in a cart and gave out a lunch tray. David fed his father some of the creamed corn, toast, cottage cheese, pear slices, and the milk. He coaxed as he held the spoon.

After lunch his father was less morose.

"Where's Steve?" he asked.

"He's at work."

"Why doesn't Steve come?"

"He's at work." David began to clean up the tray.

"They let you out of the Army?"

"Yes, Dad, two years ago."

"Why aren't you at work?"

"I don't have a job."

A nurse entered the room.

"You're lazy and stupid." His father's declaration had been made with vehemence.

The nurse looked away from David. The bedspread was suddenly a thing of great interest. David looked at it too and wished he was someplace else.

There was no place else.

***

The family sat on chairs lined against the wall that faced the casket. No one talked. The casket lid was open. If David stared long enough at the body it appeared that his father was breathing, the chest moving up and down the smallest fraction of an inch. He knew it was an illusion. Something he wanted to see.

Life had eased out of his father's body after all that pain of the last month, the month of terrible decline. The body shrinking in bed.

Someone familiar approached from the hall. She was dressed up, whoever she was...Susan. What was she doing here? Who told her to come? He hadn't. He would never. Darlene. It was Darlene. Didn't she know they weren't seeing each other anymore? God. More unpleasantness.

Susan entered the parlor and walked up to him. She looked a little nervous. Should he stand? He didn't know.

"Hello, David."

"Hello."

She sat down next to him.

"I'm sorry to hear about your father. Is there anything I can do?"

David shook his head. The room sat in silence. David knew Steve was suppressing a grin. He did not want to even look at Susan. He suppressed an urge to get up and walk out. Go to the lounge and have a cup of coffee. Be by himself. No people.

The Stephensons came, followed by the Boyds, Charlie Trenter, Evelyn Monte, and others. People talked.

It was time to do something. He turned toward her. "You been ok?"

"Yeah. You?"

David nodded yes. "Considering." He looked down at her thigh and saw her nearby hand. He thought about holding it.

"Are you making good money?"

David held his breath. Had she actually asked that? In a funeral home? With his dead father fifteen feet away? His face felt warm. What the devil did she want anyway? A Corvette? A trip to Europe? Damn her!

Did anyone hear her?

He knew who he was. What he was. He was not making good money and he never would. It wasn't in him. He was not like Steve.

David felt her steady, unapologetic stare as she waited for a reply. He got up and stood by the casket. She did not join him.

***

He had been given the task of going through his father's things. He emptied drawers, shelves, and closets. A memory of his father's existence lingered in the razors, aftershave lotions, ties, shoes, old magazines, and ancient photos. It was mysterious. The man was dead, yet his invisible shadow, his molecules, were on everything. David filled five large garbage bags. Mom wanted everything gone. It was like he was burying the man a second time as he threw away the socks, the pajamas, the shirts, belts, the man's slippers, the frayed straw hat his dad wore when he baled hay. A memory of loading the hay onto a slow-moving wagon during a sunny afternoon years, years ago came to David.

He found a letter in a shoebox that had photos, receipts, a roofing estimate, business cards from strangers, and a comb. The letter was one folded, yellowed page.

Dear Grace,

I am not much a letter writing, I am not that well schooled, but here goes. My new job is going good. I am welding. It sure is loud and noisy in the plant. The other guys don't know me too well, but I am starting to be friends with two of them, Bill and Ivan.

They call me Country. That's my name I guess. They pay is good. I hope to save enough to buy a farm someday.

I miss you every day, Grace, and I think of you all the time.

Hope you think of me from time to time.

Yours truly, Tom.

p.s. I am learning a new song on the guitar that I wrote for you.
I will play it for you if you come to the company picnic with me.
Will you come? Tom.

David smiled as he folded the half-century old paper. He put it in his pocket to later show to his mother, Grace.

***

His car was parked on an old logging road that went through the woods. His opened his fourth can of beer. The first one had a flat taste, the second was better, the third even better, the fourth one flat again. The song coming through the car radio was a ballad that plodded along. Throbbing violins echoed the singer's complaint of being unloved. David turned the radio off and kicked the dashboard.

"Nuff of that shit."

It was one a.m. He took another sip. David rolled down the window and leaned his head out. The warm air of the night felt good on his face. Something moved through the underbrush ahead. The steps were delicate, timid. David turned on the car headlights and saw a startled doe twenty feet away. The brown animal stood still in the hypnotic, white light. Her eyes looked like large, garish gems.

David turned the lights off and heard the animal bound away. He got out of the car and walked to where she had stood. He sipped from his can. He thought that being among the trees would comfort him. He needed comfort. He needed to get drunk. He sipped. They fired him! From a part-time job! He hadn't been there a month! God, what a loser he was. A part-time job! He couldn't keep anything. Why did people hate him? Because he was a loser. A loser.

He poured out the rest of the beer onto the ground.

***

He didn't want to spend the money, but he went anyway. His mother had said that he needed to get out more. So he went to the county fair and walked among the pig pens, the rows of chicken cages, and the lines of cows in the livestock shed. He was not interested in livestock. He recalled the time he showed Bessie, his heifer, and got a white ribbon. Steve had entered Jezebel and was granted Champion of Class.

The next building was the produce shed. Huge pumpkins, watermelons, cantaloupes, and ears of corn, all decorated with ribbons of blue, red, white, filled the tables. He stepped out almost immediately.

He walked over to the noisy midway. Shoulders and elbows bumped into him. The urgent part of the crowd separated as it came upon David, swerved around him, and merged together in front of him. He saw hand-holding couples whose pace was faster than his. Nearly every girl wore a halter top and skin-hugging shorts. Sandals. Some of the exposed flesh was not that attractive; some of it was. David walked by the moving Ferris wheel, the ring toss booths, the cotton candy vendors, the hot dog stands, the man who guessed your age and weight. He saw the Obese Woman. She sat on a bench and panted slightly in the summer heat. How much did she weigh? David guessed over five hundred pounds. Her flabby arms were bigger than his legs. She wore a purple dress. Sandals. A folded-up aluminum walker was nearby.

The Obese Woman looked at him. She did not care that he had been inspecting her. He saw her unrelenting boredom, her angry despair. A bead of sweat ran down her thick neck.

He walked away.

At the parking lot he saw a couple driving out in a convertible sports car. The woman in the passenger seat had thick, blonde hair. She laughed and laughed at something hilarious. David opened his car door and sat on the faded and torn fabric of the car seat. Just sat there.

***

He found his father's single-shot rifle and the shells. The aim would have to be precise to make it work. He knew that. Aim was critical. Critical. He would have to be calm. He could not miss. Could not.

David took off his shoes, removed his socks. He started to put the socks into the clothes hamper. No, he would not need them anymore. He threw them into the trash can beside his desk. He slid the shoes under the bed and lined them neatly together. He turned the radio on to mask the sound of the shot. He adjusted the volume so that it was low. He did not want to wake his mother.

David looked at his bedroom. It was neat. That sergeant in Fort Knox—what was his name—would be pleased. He had thrown away the miscellaneous, unnecessary stuff. The books, magazines, fingernail clippers, odds and ends. The clothes she could donate to Salvation Army.

It was time. He slid a shell in the firing chamber, closed the bolt, flicked the safety off, sat on the edge of the bed, put the heel of the stock of the rifle on the floor between his bare feet, leaned over, guided the end of the barrel into his mouth, held the barrel with both hands, and slipped his big toe into the trigger guard.

He listened to the *thud thud thud* of his heart.

Why was he waiting? Why was he waiting??

David closed his wet eyes. The barrel had a peculiar taste. His back began to ache.

Why was he waiting?

He heard the music on the radio. A symphony. Mozart? Haydn? He saw the rifle, the length of it, and the carpet. He realized he should have vacuumed the carpet. It wasn't clean enough.

He waited for his courage to return. The necessity of it. It would take time. He had time. He had all kinds of time before dawn. It would be over before morning. Over.

He heard the door open but did not look up. He heard the harsh gasp and could not move. When his mother's hand grabbed the barrel he still could not move.

***

His mother came out of the therapist's office. David reluctantly put down the magazine. She sat in a chair and reached into her purse for a facial tissue. He noticed that her eyes were puffy from crying. He also saw that she looked older, that she was indeed an old woman. She was not frail or withered, just worn. There were years in her body.

"Come in, David," said the therapist.

David followed the pudgy, bearded man into the office. The man motioned to a chair and David sat.

"Tell me about yourself."

"There's nothing to tell."

"I know it's difficult. Just think of me as a friend." The therapist waited.

David was silent. He could outwait the therapist.

"Your mother says you don't have any friends."

"No."

"Why is that?"

David grimaced. "I'm not well liked."

"Why?"

"I don't know."

"Are you rude? Arrogant? Obnoxious? Do you have terrific body odor?" The therapist laughed. "Are you mute? You can't speak English? No? None of those things? Can you smile? Can you listen? Yes? Then you can have friends."

David hated the therapist.

"Do you avoid people?"

David shrugged his shoulders.

"Do you like your mother?"

"Sure."

"Your father?"

"He's dead," said Adam.

"Do you miss your father?"

David considered it. He had no answer.

"Did you love him? Did he love you?"

David still had no answer. A minute passed. "When I was six he used to call me Little Dummy."

The therapist listened.

"I suppose the worst thing was when he said I was lazy and stupid."

"When did that happen?"

"When he was in the nursing home. He was right. I am stupid."

"Really? According to your mother you finished in the top ten of your graduating class."

"That doesn't mean anything."

The therapist wrote a few words on his note pad.

"How would you describe yourself using three words?"

"Unemployed. Unattractive." David could not think of a third word. "I'm not like Steve."

"Who is Steve?"

"My brother. He has a good job and a wife."

"Did your father prefer him?"

"Yes. Always."

The rest of the session passed in a realm without time. David revealed to the pudgy, bearded stranger all sorrows forgotten, truths he did not know he had buried within.

***

They talked in the car on the way back.

"It was rough at first being married to him," said his mother. "We moved out to the country. To the farm. I didn't know a soul. I was so lonely. I thought, hoped, prayed, he would take me to town once in a while, but all he did was work. He worked all the time. To build the farm up. That took years. He had the best farm around. He was so proud of that. You and Steve were a lot of help. I did not know how to drive a car. He wouldn't teach me. I taught myself in the driveway. Almost ran into the house more than once." His mother laughed.

Her tone changed. "When you were born, Tom was so proud of you. He called you his little man. One day—you were just crawling then—he had come in from the evening milking and you knew he put on his slippers after he took off his work boots. Well, you crawled after them and brought them to him. He was so pleased."

"I'm not a baby anymore, Mom. I'm not doing too well as an adult."

"You're just like your father. He was very shy. He married late. I thought he would never ask me. He was a good man. Despite the hardships. And so are you."

"What did that guy tell you what was wrong with me?"

"He said you suffer from low self-esteem and that you have a melancholic personality. I know you feel unloved, David, but you will be someday. You're going to be fine." She reached over and put her hand on his. David couldn't recall the last time she had touched him.

***

David walked into the barn. He needed to be alone. He had to think about all the things the therapist had said. He couldn't remember them all. What had that professor said in his lecture that was on public television? *One's life is a mystery. One cannot truly understand what one's life is about until most of it has been lived.* He understood that he wasn't really very smart. His dad really had been right. He had made stupid decisions. Decisions based upon hope. He had not known what the world was like. He had not known what people wanted from him. He did not know what the rules were. No one had told him.

He had lived a long time. He was still young, but he had lived a long time. Two guys he went to high school with were already dead. Dead in the ground. And he was alive. He had to learn how to live, that's all.

David saw his father's tools hanging on nails on a horizontal board on the barn wall. A framing square, a handsaw, a bow saw, a level, a crowbar, a claw hammer. He picked up the hammer. The wooden handle was worn. How old was it? Sixty years? How many nails had he driven with it? And how many had he pulled out? Yes, the man liked to work.

Oh, Dad. Why did you make it so hard to love you? Mom told me you loved me the best you knew how.

But why did you make it so hard for me to love you back?

Why?

He closed his eyes.

Why?

GARY GALSWORTH
A STEADY TRICKLE

Shouldn't I be somewhere else,
doing more than sharing
in this peace and quiet,

Working harder
at things that need to be done?

Looking at the streambed, seeing a steady
trickle passing through the sand and pebbles,
I see everything that needs doing is being done.

Galsworth

THE RAILING

Through the spindles of the porch railing
I see the driveway,
rain splashing on puddles.

Beyond those slender posts,
lined up in lean precision,
an unruly afternoon.

Galsworth

MIKE COHEN
THE CROSS AND THE WINDMILLS

Coming over a low hill on the Texas plains east of Amarillo, driving Interstate 40, one sees on the horizon a white cross. The town nearby is Groom, with about six hundred residents, located on a bypass from the interstate, a little piece of the old Route 66. The cross, when it suddenly appeared on the horizon and grew gradually bigger as one approached, was until recently an imposing and isolated sight, dominating an otherwise empty landscape. Since the cross is visible for fifteen or twenty miles, there is a lot of time for the traveler to wonder at its presence, to speculate on exactly how big it is and who erected it. The answers to these questions may be found by pulling into the small park next to the cross and reading the information posted there.

The cross is almost 60 meters high—190 feet to be exact, or as tall as a 19-story building. Its arms stretch 110 feet. For comparison, the statue of *Christ the Redeemer* that looks out over Rio de Janeiro from the top of Corcovado Mountain is only 30 meters tall, though it has the advantage of Corcovado's 700-meter height to give it prominence. The stylized corrugations representing folds in the robe in Paul Landowski's Art Deco design for *Cristo Redentor* may possibly have suggested the fluting or channeling in the skin of the Groom cross. Two Texas millionaires are responsible for the cross. Chris Britten, who owned the large, now defunct gas station, curio shop, and restaurant nearby, donated the land, and Steve Thomas had the cross built in sections in Pampa, Texas, before it was transported and assembled at this site in 1995. Bronze statues representing the stations of the cross and other sacred subjects ring the white metal cross. These include a pietá copied from Michelangelo, a St. Michael and Lucifer that could be mistaken for St. George and the Dragon, a fountain, an empty tomb, an anti-abortion monument, and the ten commandments. But the main player is the cross, dwarfing all the bronze below. Yet it is almost an anticlimax to arrive at the cross, since we can only imagine its size, with nothing to provide scale, during our approach to it, and it could, for all we could guess from ten or five miles away, be 400 feet tall.

Not long ago as I drove on I-40, approaching the cross at Groom, I saw on the horizon white shapes of a very different sort, dozens of them, and all larger than the Groom cross. They were the huge three-bladed windmills or wind turbines that we have become accustomed to seeing over the last few years on the windy plains of America. Cross and turbines have in common a certain mysteriousness of scale: I find it difficult, even when I am within a few hundred yards, to guess how large they are. But I have often seen on the road trucks transporting the blades of turbines, and with cars for comparison I have no trouble comprehending that each blade is over a hundred feet long.

In fact the blades are 130 feet long, and the tower that supports them is over 250 feet high, so the structure, when a blade is pointing straight up, is easily 400 feet tall, or more than twice the height of the Groom cross, and there are dozens of them in view as one approaches and drives by the cross. The wind turbines (so-called even though they are not actually turbines but simple generators powered by the geared-up turning of a wind fan) are often arranged along the fronts of mesas so that they look like modern equivalents of the windmills of La Mancha, so that I can imagine some wizard—Frestón, for instance—had replaced the old landmarks with these three-armed white giants. Wind farms, they call these collections, and some in America have almost 5,000 of the turbines.

I have to think that at least part of the intent and effort of the two millionaires who put up the cross has been frustrated. The intent, I imagine, was at least partly to create a particular moment of contemplation of Christianity's central symbol and of what it means to those speeding toward it over the plains of the Texas Panhandle at 75 miles an hour. Whether our thoughts were contemplative and religious, or whether, like me, you were merely marveling at the scale of the cross, it captured your thoughts for the time it took to reach it. It gestured upward from a terrain of flatness and clear views to a far horizon. Like Wallace Stevens's jar in Tennessee, the cross organized a natural landscape with the insertion of a man-made object and perhaps pointed thoughts toward a third realm beyond the physical.

But no more. What has happened here is partly dilution and distraction. Attention that once had been trained solely on the cross is now divided among a number of monumental shapes on the plain. An added distraction is the movement of the new shapes. An aesthetic question arises: is the cross more beautiful than the windmills, or vice versa? And beyond aesthetics is the question of meaning and meaningful activity: the cross does symbolic work while the wind turbines do real work. The many questions the turbines raise do not touch the metaphysical. Who put them up? Where does the electricity they generate get distributed, and how much juice is there? Does the wind always blow here? How long does it take for the electricity generated to pay off the cost of these huge machines? Wind turbines bring us to the things of this world.

ANNETTE VELASQUEZ
HAG AS GODDESS

To recognize the beauty of the
crone
and regard the hag as goddess—
seems ludicrous
revolutionary at the least,
a wild leaping

(cont)

from current trends,
so-called sensibilities.
For today, it is youth that is celebrated
the smooth face,
a model's slimness,
gleaming teeth
and abundant hair-
these are the only ideals
coveted and emulated—
revered.
Age is equated with decline,
undesirable
—more so in a woman….
But,
ancient foremothers,
indigenous people everywhere—
you
know
the value and wisdom
of the grandmothers
healers and comforters
storytellers and teachers
nurturers deeply knowing….
Women much-loved
vital players in life's
perpetual spin
aged women,
central in nature's dance
partaking
in the cycles and rhythms
of birth and blossoming
growth and maturation ripening,
magical women….
We must remember
and celebrate
the matriarchs
and matrons
yesterday's maidens
now menopausal,
but always magnificent.

Velasquez

MEREDITH TREDE
BRING HIM HOME

News clippings, notebooks, folders, post-its:
a jumble of fear. My words won't cohere.

What if something I say should slow him down,
lead him to hesitate

a tick of time,
and the other, the other, doesn't wait?

They took him today to photograph his tattoos.
Honor engraved on the tender underside

of his left forearm, a string of rosary beads
encircling his upper right arm,

on his chest *Thy will be done.*
His best friend dreamt of tossing, turning,

and waking to find his blanket folded
into an American flag triangle.

Sometimes they've said he wouldn't go.
Now the Marines have told him so, and so

whose child will be the one to go?
Bring them home.

Trede

J P DALEY
PEG OF HIS HEART

Back in the early '60s a double-wide house trailer was towed onto an empty lot on the north side of Route 72. During the next eight months the trailer was converted into the Tick Tock Diner, all metal and glass with a large clock outlined in blue neon over the entrance. At the time, Route 72 was just a single lane road. Today, almost seventeen years later, that same road has become a major highway with three lanes in each direction, bypassing the small town of Apple Creek. And now, before summer's end, the Tick Tock will be torn down to make way for a 7-Eleven Mini-Mart.

When the rumor first circulated around Apple Creek about the demise of the Tick Tock, Peggy Rhodes, in her mid-thirties with head-turning good looks, wrote to the 7-Eleven home office. She boasted of her nearly twelve years of waitressing, emphasizing her exceptional people skills and impressive work ethic. But she was turned down. All positions at the Apple Creek 7-Eleven would be filled by employees from other franchises.

*   *   *

On a bitter cold January afternoon, made even more uncomfortable by the sharp wind coming out of the northwest, Scratch O'Connor limped his way into the Tick Tock, as he did every day at two o'clock.

"Coffee?" asked Peg.

"Yeah, an' let me have one of them crullers." He lowered himself onto a stool and hooked his cane on the counter's edge. "Any luck with your job search, Peg?"

"Not yet. Things are slow after the holidays."

"I thought fer sure them folks at 7-Eleven would have snapped you up. Hell, who's better at waitin' on folks than you?"

"Experience don't mean nothing no more." She set down his coffee and pastry. "Companies want the young ones. They don't have to pay 'em as much."

"Humph. Kids today don't stay in one place long enough to get any experience." He sipped his coffee and tore off a piece of cruller. "Hell, I had thirty-two years with the railroad 'fore I banged up this knee of mine."

"I'll tell you something else," Peggy added. "Companies love it when the young ones move on. That way, they don't get no pensions or any of the other stuff." She added a fresh layer of frosted-pink lipstick, adjusted her breasts, checked her reflection in the sliding glass door of the dessert case, then took menus over to the two contractors in the booth by the window.

"Whoa," shouted Nick Sparrow as he stepped into the diner, clapping his gloved hands. "Getting nippy out there. When that sun goes down, I'm gonna freeze off my most wonderful things." Tall and thin and wearing a black Stetson hat, he shuffled over to the counter. "Hey, Old Timer, you want to move yer goddamn cane so someone else can sit down?" he said with a broad smile as he took the stool next to Scratch.

"Whudda ya say, Nicky-boy?" He laughed and patted Nick's shoulder. "What brings ya out this way?"

"Gotta pick up a load of auto parts at the terminal out in west New York an' take 'em back to the Bronx."

"Well, yer in luck, they're callin' fer clear weather. No snow or nothin'."

"Yeah, but that friggin' cold gets t'ya. An' the truck's heater ain't that great."

"Get yerself some Jack Daniels, that'll keep ya warm." He added a short laugh and finished his coffee. "Did ya hear this place'll be no more come Labor Day?"

"Yeah, one of the guys back at the garage told me."

"Thing is, Peggy needs a job. And yours truly needs to find another place to have his afternoon coffee." He held up his empty cup until Peggy hurried over with a refill.

"Hi, Nick, coffee?"

"Thanks, darlin'." He leaned forward to get a better look down her blouse. "Hey, Scratch, tell me something. How the hell you ever get that name? You never said." He watched Peggy sway her way to the other end of the counter, convinced she added a little extra for his benefit.

"My given name's Michael. Scratch I got by majority rule."

"Whudda ya mean?"

"Well ya see...." He sipped his coffee and smiled like he had won a hand at poker. "Late one afternoon, in my junior year at Lincoln High, Alice McGuire and me went out behind the school. She had cigarettes and I had a small bottle of Green River. Hell, one thing led to another. We got to rolling around in what we thought was a bunch of grass and leaves. Next morning in the shower, after gym class, I looked down at a bunch of ugly red scratches. So did all the guys in my class. That's how I got the name. And it stuck."

*   *   *

Scratch glanced at the clock over the entrance to the kitchen. Two minutes to four. Although Cedar Manor wasn't that far from the diner, he had to get back by four-thirty, in time for meds. He finished his coffee and grabbed his cane.

"Peg, see ya t'morrow. Nicky-boy, catch ya next time." He pulled the door closed.

Scratch O'Conner had been a resident at Cedar Manor since retiring from Western New York Railroad, twelve years ago. As an ex-employee of the Manor's most generous benefactor, he was allowed to leave the grounds without a chaperone.

"God, I'm gonna miss that guy," said Peg. "He's been coming in here every afternoon since the day I started." She stood at the door and watched the old man limp across the parking lot.

"More coffee, Nick?"

"Yeah, an' let me have a burger. Medium, with lots of fries. Where ya been lookin' fer work?"

"Pretty much any place dealing with food and people." She cleared the counter where Scratch had been sitting and put the dollar in her apron.

"How about me? Think ya could deal with me, darlin'?" Nick pushed his hat back and held out his arms as if to say, *take me I'm yours.*

"You're okay—for a customer." She pushed her way into the kitchen.

Nick struggled out of his leather jacket. Harley-Davidson was printed in orange across the front of his black tee shirt. Tattoos of naked women covered both arms.

"Did you want onions on that?" she asked as she returned with a bottle of ketchup and put down a placemat.

"Yeah, lots of 'em. Ya know, I might have something fer ya. You've got a car, right—I mean a way of getting around?"

"If you're talking about Meals-On-Wheels, forget it."

"No, uh, uh, hold on. Ever hear of the Remote Coyote? It's down in Yonkers. Owner's a friend of mine. He's always looking for good help."

"That's quite a trip, Nick."

"Twenty, thirty miles at most. What's the big deal?" He swiped black stringy hair off his forehead. "Think about it, Peg. You'd make more in tips in one night at the Coyote than you would in this joint in a week."

"I don't know. I'd like to stay around here. What kind of place is it?" She set down his burger.

"Like a sports bar, only high-end—great food and music. You'd do terrific in this place." He grabbed the burger, bit off a mouthful, then licked at the ketchup sliding down his hand. "Tell ya what. I'll be down in Yonkers in a week or so." He continued chewing. "I'll stop by and tell Anthony—he's the owner—what a good looker you are and how hard working."

If I can get her down there to meet him, he thought as his eyes swept over her snug-fitting blouse, *maybe he'll lighten up on the money I owe.*

* * *

The following Wednesday afternoon, Scratch O'Connor took his usual place at the counter. An elderly man, sitting alone in a booth waved, then went back to reading the papers with a magnifying glass. Scratch watched Peg as she moved from one customer to another, encouraging conversation and laughter, or at least a smile.

"Hi, Scratch," she said as she set down a cruller and poured his coffee. "Guess what? Contractors were in here earlier with a couple of the 7-Eleven people."

"Problem?"

"No, but forget Labor Day. They want to be up and running by July 4th weekend."

"Makes sense, Peg. That's a big holiday for them. Lots of folks on the road."

"Yeah, but that cuts into the time I got to find another job." She sampled a small piece of his cruller. "My apartment lease is up at the end of April. I don't know if I should renew or not."

"Plenty of time. Don't worry. I'm sure something will turn up. Just keep lookin'."

* * *

Located on a narrow side street not far from the Hudson River, the Remote Coyote attracted very little attention by design. The single story, windowless brick building shared the block with an overgrown vacant lot. There was no signage of any kind, but fastened to the dark oak front door, just below the peephole, was a highly polished brass silhouette of a grinning coyote. Nick had called earlier to make sure Anthony would be available if he stopped by before the place opened at four o'clock.

He pulled up behind a black Lincoln Town Car. The Coyote front door swung open before he could knock. Bruno stood in the way: six feet four, 340 pounds, completely bald and dressed in black, a gold ring in each ear. "He's in the back." He jerked his thumb and stepped aside.

The sharp smell of disinfectant stung Nick's nose as he crossed the dimly lit room. Over by the lap dance area, a thin, middle-aged man on his hands and knees continued scrubbing the floor. Red lights shined down on an oval stage; three shiny brass poles reached from floor to ceiling. Nick walked down a long narrow hallway on the far side of the room and knocked on the door marked Private.

"Yeah, c'mon, it's open." Cautiously, Nick stepped inside. "Before you say one word, how much ya got?" Anthony pushed his sleeve back and held out his hand.

"I'll have somethin' next week. Swear to God, Anthony. I promise ya. Now wait'll ya see the girl I got fer ya. She's gorgeous, mid-thirties, with a set of jugs the size of eggplants." He reached out, hands cupped as visual aids. "An' she's terrific with people."

"What's she doing now?"

"She's a waitress. A real find."

"Nick!" Anthony smacked the top of his desk, sending an ashtray and pencils tumbling to the floor. "How many fuckin' times I gotta tell ya? I don't need no goddamn waitresses. I need pole dancers—broads who'll go topless. She gonna do that?"

"Not a problem." Nick mumbled, wiping sweat from his upper lip. "I told her about this place, Anthony. Told her she could make a lot of dough. She's really excited."

"What's her name?"

"Peggy Rhodes. You're gonna love her, Anthony."

"Get her down here. Let's see what she's got." He adjusted his gold necklace and leaned forward. "Nick, listen to me. When you come back with that broad, I want all of it—every goddam dollar, or I'll have Bruno drive you home. Because you ain't gonna be able to fuckin' walk."

*　　　*　　　*

Late Tuesday afternoon, before the Tick Tock turned busy serving dinner, Peg relaxed at the counter with a cup of coffee. She looked up at the clock. *I can't remember when he didn't show up for his afternoon coffee.* She looked over her shoulder every time the door swung open to see if it was Scratch. Two weeks passed and she hadn't heard from him. Then early one morning, as she busied herself serving a crowd of impatient commuters, he called.

"Whuddaya say, pretty person?"

"Scratch! Where are you?" She untangled the phone cord and stepped away from the counter. "Are you okay?"

"I'm gonna make it."

"Make it? Make what? Where are you?"

"Not to worry. I'm back here at the Manor with my new knee," he said with a nervous laugh. "Fell in the goddamn shower an' put the finishing touches on that bum knee of mine."

"You're okay, right? I mean, you didn't hit your head or nothing, did you?"

"Nah. An' the doc said the surgery went well."

"I was really worried." She took a deep breath steadying herself. "I didn't know where you were."

"I'll be okay, but I'm gonna miss my afternoons at the diner. An' ya know, Peg, I'm gonna miss you even more. You've been such a good friend to this old man—more like a daughter."

"I'm just so glad you're safe," she sniffed as she touched her apron to the corners of her eyes.

"Hey, enough about me. Any luck with your job search?"

"Not yet. But you know Nick, the truck driver? He wants me to meet a friend of his. Said he owns a sports bar kind of place down in Yonkers. The Roving Coyote or something like that."

"Remote Coyote," Scratch corrected. "You ever been there?"

"Uh, uh. I don't know if I want to travel that far. But ya know, there's not much happening around here."

"Tell ya what. I sure could use a visitor after all that time in the hospital. Why don't ya come over to the Manor on yer day off? I'll treat ya to lunch in the new dining room. It's been completely remodeled."

*   *   *

A large canvas-covered trailer truck pulled into the parking lot next to the diner. Nick turned off the engine and rested his forehead on the steering wheel while drumming nervously on the dashboard. Once again, he had let himself slide into an unhealthy situation. He promised Anthony he'd get back to him over a week ago. And he didn't. He was supposed to bring Peggy down for her interview and pay Anthony all the money he owed. Now two weeks had passed and the most Nick had pulled together was six hundred bucks—a third of what he needed. *Can't waste any more time,* he thought. *Gotta get her down there. Maybe Anthony'll cut me some slack when he sees how well-built she is.*

"Hi, Peg," said Nick as he walked over and sat at the counter.

"Coffee?" She held up the pot.

"Yeah, but I can't stay long. Look, it's all set for you at the Coyote. My friend Anthony can't wait to meet you." He leaned over and slurped his coffee canine-style. "Suppose I pick you up tomorrow afternoon, say around two."

"No, Nick. I can't just walk out of here like that. Besides, I promised the owner I'd work late tomorrow."

"What time you finish up? I'll come by around …. "

"Nick," she cut in, "I'm still not sure I want to work all the way down in Yonkers."

"Peg, check it out at least. Meet my friend. See what he's got to offer. Yer gonna love the place. An' remember, you can make a lot of money at the Coyote."

She freshened another customer's coffee, then turned back to Nick. "Okay, I'll go. But I can't until the end of next week."

"Ah, c'mon, Peg, cut the bullshit, will ya." He dug in his pocket. "Here's my number. When yer done screwin' around, give me a call." He threw two quarters on the counter and stomped to the door

*   *   *

When she stepped into the lobby of Cedar Manor, Scratch rolled his wheelchair over. "Well, well, well, look at you. How've ya been, Peg?" he said with a broad smile, his eyes bright.

"I'm good, but what about you?" She leaned over and kissed his forehead. "Mmm, you smell nice. How's your knee?"

"Ahh, I think the worst is over." His shirtsleeves were rolled back on his forearms. Khaki shorts ended just above the soft cast and bandages covering his right knee. "C'mon, dining room's down this way." He pointed across the lobby.

Large enough to host an elaborate wedding reception, the dining room had been completely done over and no longer had that cafeteria look. The walls had been painted bright blue replacing the institutional green and faded yellow. Oil paintings of the Hudson River Valley hung alongside each window. Round tables of different sizes, draped in white linen, filled the room.

"Gee, this is really something. Very impressive," she said as she steered his wheelchair to a table next to a window.

"Yeah, they did a pretty good job."

She removed her jacket and sat across from him.

"You look so different without your uniform and apron, Peggy—very nice."

"Well, thank you." Her complexion blended with her pink blouse. "You've lived here quite a while, haven't you, Scratch?"

"Thirteen years come October." He hesitated before turning the conversation. "By the way, have you interviewed for that job in Yonkers?"

"Not yet. Nick wanted to take me down there the other day. But I couldn't go. He wasn't too happy about that," she shrugged. "But I promised my boss I'd help out after one of the other girls left to work at McDonald's."

Scratch leaned across the table and held her hands. "For just a few moments, Peggy, pretend I'm your father."

"I've done that a few times," she said with a warm smile.

"Well listen to me, then," his expression sober. "I don't want you down there. You're nothing like that place. The Remote Coyote is a strip joint, a dive. They'd have you parading around half-naked while a bunch of lowlifes shouted ugly remarks and tossed money at ya."

"What, no! I wouldn't …." She put both hands to her face. "I'd never …."

"That place has always been like that—a human dump. I don't know how many times it's changed hands. Used to be called the Raccoon Saloon."

"Really. Are you kidding?"

He squeezed her hand. "Pay attention to what I'm tellin' ya. Don't get involved with those people. Not ever." He settled back in his wheelchair.

"Good afternoon, Mr. O'Connor," said a middle-aged woman as she walked over to his table and pulled up a chair. "How's the knee?"

"Hey, whudda ya say, Laura. It's comin' along. Another week an' I get rid of this wheelchair." An awkward silence followed while everyone looked around wondering who would speak first.

"Is this the young lady you've been telling me about?"

"I'd like you to meet my very dear friend, Miss Peggy Rhodes. The most caring, people person on the eastern seaboard," he said beaming. "Peg, say hi to Laura Prescott, Cedar Manor's Food & Beverage director." The two women exchanged greetings. "I'll let you ladies get acquainted," he said, wheeling his chair over to an empty table.

"I'm assuming Mr. O'Connor already told you we'd be adding a couple of new employees to our dining room staff once the renovations were completed."

"No, he didn't," said Peg. "He didn't tell me I'd be meeting with you today, either."

"Typical O'Connor," said Laura as she rolled her eyes while slowly shaking her head. "When I visited him in the hospital we agreed the three of us would meet for lunch today. He first started telling me about you right after the holidays, when it was announced that 7-Eleven bought the Tick Tock Diner. And he's been telling me about you at least once a week ever since.

"I've already added two young people to the dining room waitstaff. I really could use another, but he or she would have to be very experienced. Someone who can make sure the dining room runs smoothly and efficiently. It's very important that meals at Cedar Manor provide an enjoyable dining experience for our residents."

Peg sat still, listening closely.

"Keep in mind," Laura continued, "the residents at Cedar Manor are elderly. Many of them have health issues. They are wonderful people, but they can be demanding and at times extremely impatient."

Why is she telling me all this? What did Scratch say to her? Peg wondered as she wrung her hands under the table.

"If you'd like to be considered, let's meet next Friday morning. Say 9:15 in my office?"

"Fine, I'd like that," said Peg.

"I want the new person on board before the end of May." Laura paused as she buttoned her blazer. "It's been very nice meeting you. I look forward to Friday. Mr. Le Clair, the Manor's chef, will join us." She shook hands and excused herself, then walked over to Scratch's table.

"What do you think?" he asked.

"She seems very nice. We'll see." She winked and headed toward the lobby.

*   *   *

A week after her interview, Peg still hadn't heard from anyone at Cedar Manor. She sat staring at her coffee cup, wondering. *Maybe they left a message on my home phone. Why haven't I heard from Scratch? Could it be I didn't get the job and he's too embarrassed to call?*

The amber lights of a familiar looking eighteen-wheeler caught her attention as it pulled into the parking lot. The driver, barrel-chested and a few inches over five feet, wore a denim jacket and dungarees. He left the truck idling and hurried into the diner.

"Hi, welcome to the Tick Tock," said Peg. "Coffee?"

"Yeah, an' a menu." He sat at the counter.

"You know a guy named Nick Sparrow?" she asked as she filled his cup. "He drives a truck same as yours. Comes in here every so often."

"That's his truck," he jerked his thumb over his shoulder. "I'm fillin' in for 'im."

"He go on vacation, or something?" She set down a menu.

"Nah, I was told he took a pretty bad fall."

"Really? Is he okay?"

"Well, he won't be drivin' that truck for a while. Broke his leg.

Also broke his nose. Lost a couple of teeth and his left ear had to be sewn back in place."

"Oh my, God. How did all that happen?" she stepped back, hands to her face.

"Not sure. All they told me at the garage was that he fell down a flight of stairs at the train station. Maybe he was going on vacation. Who knows?"

*   *   *

The following afternoon, just before two o'clock, an Apple Creek taxi with more dents than rust pulled up in front of the Tick Tock Diner. The driver jumped out and helped Scratch adjust his crutches, then watched the old man make his way up the handicapped ramp into the diner.

"Scratch!" shouted Peg, causing heads to turn as she hurried from behind the counter. She hugged her longtime friend, kissed his cheek and helped him into a booth. "I got it! I got the job! Mrs. Prescott called me at home. Did she tell you?"

"Yeah, just this morning. Congratulations!"

"I can't believe it. I'm so excited." She leaned his crutches in the corner. "I was so nervous when Mrs. Prescott called. She told me all you did—even about the letter of recommendation. I just wish there were some way I could do something for you."

"You always have, Peg."

JENNIE WHITE
**A FILM ABOUT MENSTRUAL EQUALITY WON AN OSCAR AND
I APOLOGIZED TO MY MOTHER FOR THE ACCEPTANCE
SPEECH**

"I'm not crying because I'm on my period or anything."
—Rayka Zehtabchi

My mother
crosses her arms
at the winner's comment
and huffs with
a white-knuckled intensity
strong enough to tell me
she does not approve of
this woman.   (cont)

I'm tempted to mention
that's what their film is about,
but a winner on the screen
does not mean I'll win the fight
with her sense of God-given grace.

Fights aren't
won by golden
men held by gown-clad
women on a tube TV,
tied or entangled
woman or object.

Fights are won in everyday places
in everyday ways,
not caring
who sees me scrutinize tampons at Wal-Mart
or if people see the pad in my hand
instead of up my sleeve.

Fights can be won in living rooms,
telling my mom that women deserve
to mention our periods.

But I'm so tired tonight,
too tired to fight, so
I adjust the laptop I'm using as
a heating pad for my cramps,
agree with her
and apologize.

White

BABY?

The door closed,
muttered "damnit"s
soft whining "no"s
the sounds of
unroll
      ing

(cont)

un
roll
ing
un
roll
ing
and wrappingwrapp
ingwrapping
escape through
the door jamb.

I rattle my knuckles
on fiberboard,
and ask "Baby?
Everything ok?"
Her "yeah"s quaver
then break.

Head cradled on
the bathtub's rim,
she looks like
the pulled plug
drained her too.

Toilet paper peeks out
under her shorts' hem.

I ask again, the same
but altogether different,
"Baby?"

She reaches for
my hand, swaddles it
in her t-shirt and answers
"No."

White

WILLIAM HART
WHAT DO YOU WANT TO BE?

Early spring semester all ninth graders at Roosevelt were given a job preference test. We were told it could predict the sort of work that might best suit us as adults. Sounded worth a try. My parents had made me feel so secure that by age fifteen I'd felt no need to think seriously about my adult career. My taste for argumentation had convinced the folks I'd make a good attorney—and being an attorney sounded okay to me. As I saw it, I'd pull in enough bucks to live the way I wanted and would get respect. That's why when people asked what I wanted to be, I usually said "a lawyer." But I was far from sure of that and thought the test might point me to some field I hadn't yet considered, one that really grabbed me.

The psychological pigeonholing device consisted of about a hundred questions all of which asked me to make a choice between two different activities. Here's a typical question: "Would you rather (a) write a letter to a friend or (b) plant a tree?" I answered as honestly as I could though sometimes it wasn't easy. There seemed to be a lot of redundancy built into the questions and I felt more than once that I might be going against a choice I'd made earlier. It also bothered me that I was tending to choose outdoor pursuits in nature over indoor pursuits among people. While I liked fishing in the woods well enough, I really didn't think I wanted a career with the National Park Service. We were not told how or when we'd learn the test results.

Months later, ninth graders were encouraged to sign up for appointments with Mr. Sondergard, Roosevelt's guidance counselor. Here it is, I thought. He's going to tell us how the test read our vocational tea leaves. The appointments were in the evening and we could come alone or bring our parents. My mother and father wanted to go of course. Katy's parents were busy, so she signed up for the conference after mine and we gave her a ride. I was a little surprised she wanted an appointment. She and I had never discussed careers and I'd assumed she didn't have a professional one in mind. On the trip to Roosevelt though she seemed upbeat and bright with anticipation, more so than me. When I asked her about it she admitted she wanted to know the test results but wouldn't tell me what career she was interested in. I knew not to push.

Mr. Sondergard welcomed my parents and me into his office and offered us seats. He settled in behind his desk and began complimenting me on my fine record at Roosevelt. Using too many words he said that based on my grades and my standardized test scores and the comments of my teachers I could be "anything I wanted to be." Just the kind of praise parents love to hear and a glance at my mother's face told me she'd heard. Dad looked pleased too. And why not? His son could be anything he wanted: doctor, lawyer, merchant, chief, physicist, cop, bouncer, thief—anything at all! Not long after that Mr. Sondergard ushered us out of his office and that's when I realized he wasn't going to tell me the results of the job preference test. Nor had we discussed careers in any meaningful way. What exactly had been the reason for the conference—or for the test?

A glorious prairie sunset was fading to twilight over downtown as I waited in the car with my parents for Katy to return from her conference. When she climbed in the back seat and sat down next to me I saw her hopeful look was gone. She was in such a bad mood I knew better than to poke around in it. We rode in silence for a while, then she surprised me by asking what Mr. Sondergard had told me.

"He said I can be anything I want."

"Didn't he tell you what you'd be good at?"

"No."

"What else?"

"He congratulated me on my grades and stuff."

"That's all?"

I said it was. Then I asked what he'd said to her. She wouldn't tell me. Whatever it was had discouraged her enough that she'd decided to hold it balled up inside among the million other things she was holding inside. I was used to it. That was my Katy!

Over the years I've thought many times about that strange evening. Today it seems to me I must have put Mr. Sondergard in a difficult position. How could he explain to my parents and me that based on my test-determined interests I'd be happiest herding elk in Yellowstone? Given the values of the school system he represented that would have been pretty much impossible. I think he took the safe route, blowing smoke while leaving it up to me to pick a career. Maybe he realized that no test or person could predict the future of such a quirky kid.

In Katy's case, I'd guess our counselor miscalculated simply because he knew too little about her. She wouldn't have signed up to see him if she hadn't aspired to a profession of some kind. Unfortunately he had only three ways to assess her ability to succeed at a profession—her B grades, her probably so-so test scores, and the evaluations of her teachers at Robinson, the junior high she'd recently transferred out of. It's unlikely Mr. Sondergard knew her teachers there. Based on what he had, he must have assumed my girlfriend's intelligence and motivation were too pedestrian for the career her test results pointed to. The biggest strike against her would have been her gender. In 1960, girls weren't often encouraged to think about careers.

The Katy Linsey Mr. Sondergard didn't know, but that I knew, was a dedicated and focused competitor with a record of success. What had enabled her as a skate racer to take second at nationals in her age division the summer before, beyond athletic ability, was her strong motivation. It was in her nature to always try her hardest. I think she wanted to show everyone (including herself) that she could rise above any perceived shortcomings in her background and stand on her own accomplishments. Over the years I've noticed that personalities like hers usually do well in adult life—so she likely would have thrived in any career she chose. I could certainly see her as a nurse, a profession wide open to women at the time.

My memories of that evening are among my saddest because I believe I witnessed one of the major defeats of Katy's life—the plowing under of her career dream. Her family was not well off or super supportive like mine. She knew it was up to her to make something of herself and no doubt that's why by age fourteen she'd thought carefully about what she wanted to be. She'd picked her future career and had evidently set her heart on it, only to learn she lacked the right stuff to pursue it, at least according to our counselor.

Mr. Sondergard's aim in both our cases must have been to guide us onto the paths that would take us through high school and beyond. He steered me away from Yellowstone by keeping me on the academic track that led through good colleges to the professions, much in line with the goals of the honors program. And I think he steered Katy, who was less academically promising but certainly pretty, onto the path travelled by future receptionists and secretaries. His advice to her wouldn't have mattered so much if my girlfriend had had other career guides but she had none that I know except her older sister, who was a teen herself, and maybe her dad, a car salesman. I think Katy was left with a single inadequate map for her future. Being who she was she would have followed that map earnestly and with a steady purpose into a vocation much different than she'd hoped for.

KATHLEEN MCGOOKEY
YOU HAVE NOTHING TO BE AFRAID OF, ANYMORE—

Not even silver tanker trucks hauling liquid manure up and down the dirt road in regular rotation, spreading dust and stink through the air, or cancer growing lush and unbridled in your pancreas though you've always felt just fine, or the silvery seductive gaze of the phone in your son's palm, better than a lover because he can tickle it awake anytime, or the broken branch that has dangled for months in the crook of the aspen, above the flowerbed where the bearded iris are just beginning to stir, it's spring after all and someone has to pull weeds. There's time, you think, there must be time because it's spring and the swallows are singing though it's already midday, there's time to crumple a chocolate wrapper and offer it like fool's gold to the trash collectors, time to close your eyes while a nurse draws your blood into a labeled vial, your ears ringing, enough time to blow an eyelash from your fingertip—but under these circumstances, what would a wish matter?

McGookey

MARTIN H LEVINSON
NOTES FROM AN OBSESSIVE DIRECTOR

Act I, Scene 1

Larkin enters the room, fiddling with change in his right pants' pocket. The fiddling should be done in the key of D Minor, as the piece Larkin is pocket-playing is Bach's Violin Partita No. 2. He then walks stage right, however if the actor playing Larkin is a liberal and objects to anything that has to do with the word "right," he can walk stage left. Actually, it really doesn't matter which way Larkin walks as long as he remains in the general vicinity of the stage. If he doesn't do that and walks out of the theater, the other actors should do their best to improvise his part.

After Larkin finishes his stroll, a perambulation that hopefully hasn't taken too long—as the more Larkin walks the less Larkin talks—he comes upon Miranda, a millennial from Manhattan who is imbibing a mojito and munching M&M's. Alternatively, she can be sipping a sangria and snacking on a Snickers Bar. Or, she can be downing a daiquiri and feasting on a piece of fudge. On second thought, maybe she shouldn't drink or eat anything, as drinking and eating are not relevant to the scene and if she drinks and eats she may get a stomachache during the performance. With that in mind, forget the drinking and eating. Have Miranda put on some lipstick, fuss with her hair, or make a phone call instead.

When Miranda finishes her stage business a bird flies south across the stage whistling *Dixie*. It is important that the bird flies south, as it is a snowbird looking for some confederates to have fun with in Florida, hence a compass should be used to get the direction right. While having the bird fly south and whistling a Civil War song may pose a challenge to the animal trainer who has been hired for the show, please no whining about that. Just get it done.

Act I, Scene 2

At center stage moss is growing, which is very odd as the stage manager has been told a million times to get rid of the goddamned moss. That this guy still draws a salary when he can't obey simple directives is beyond me. Maybe the idiot should be fired and someone else should be hired to do away with the moss.

Back to center stage. Have the new stage manager replace the moss with a Sherman tank. Not a real tank of course, because real tanks are expensive and they can be dangerous if someone gets inside one and fires off a round or two. At this point in the play we don't want to kill off the audience; at the end of the play however, if the crowd is jeering and booing, that may be a different story.

Act II, Scene 1

At the beginning of the scene, when Larkin tries to talk to Miranda and is interrupted by the sound of breaking news on FOX TV saying that the Messiah has come down from heaven and is in New York City, where he is sitting on an A train, which has been stuck in a subway tunnel for over two hours, make sure the sound is up loud enough for everyone in the auditorium to hear the breaking story. Keep the sound at that level so the audience will also have no problem hearing the character playing Sean Hannity, who right after the news announcement comes on air and says, "The Messiah should have hired a limo to get around because the New York City subway system, like the rest of the city, is a god-awful mess filled with the meek—you know, illegals, the homeless, individuals making a minimum wage—who it seems are about to inherit the earth."

Before Sean can begin his next sentence, the twenty-two smoke machines that are on the stage should be turned on full blast to replicate the apocalypse that comes with the coming of the Messiah. There ought to be enough smoke to asphyxiate at least the first two rows of the audience, which will contribute to the pandemonium that will break out as the theater turns into a hell, to accentuate that effect the doors of the building need to be locked so the audience cannot escape. Just when everyone thinks all is lost, the stage door should be opened to let in a few first responders. (The hearings that will inevitably follow from this spectacle will doubtlessly result in legislation that will prohibit smoke machines in theaters and that's a good thing, because smoke machines are devilish devices that ought to be banned from the boards.)

IMPORTANT NOTE

During the whole performance the curtain should be raised and lowered every five to ten seconds. There are several reasons for this. First, if an actor forgets a line or two they can wait until the curtain is down to have the words given to them by the prompter or another actor. Second, with the curtain rolling up and down constantly, audience members will never know when it's time for the intermission so they may hedge their bets by leaving their seats more than once to go to the concession stand for refreshments. Third, people in need of a bathroom break can head to the loo whenever they feel like it. Finally, up-and-down-curtain raising during an entire show has never been done before and for that reason alone it's worth a shot.

A Concluding Comment

Each night when the play closes, everybody in the company should get together immediately afterward to discuss whether they have been following these notes. This may be a bit of a drag but this play is my baby and it's been loaned to the group for safekeeping so I hope everyone in the cast will keep it safe from ignorant and self-centered people who think they know more than me. For those in the company who comply with my instructions, I hope you metaphorically "break a leg" in the production of this play. To those geniuses who try to interpose their own staging and ideas, I hope you really do break a leg, and every other limb in your wretched and pathetic body. Just kidding. Not.

MICHAEL SANDLER
WISHBONE

When clearing the Thanksgiving dishes
one of us chides, *Shouldn't we save it?,*
and lets it dry, chalking time, a forked
destiny in the kitchen window.
By week's end, a fetish well-cured:
our faces close above its arch
we lever resolve thumb to thumb
as if trying to break a weld—
a seam delicate as pure gold,
ore that was *ours* could crumble
to fragmentation *mines*...
Clavicles Nature has
joined
why pull them asunder?
At times we've walked abreast
not bickering, not making up,
tensile moments wondering who would give, until some
stress sensor
in each of us flashed a *Back off!*
So why attack this brittle coupling
hoping my partner comes up short?
Just as it snaps, I blow a wish
to return to a festive table
decked with gourds, unblemished pears,
and plattered meat with no bone to pick.

Sandler

LAURA BERNSTEIN-MACHLAY
BARGAINS

I don't love the big boxes, but some bargains can't be ignored. For instance, after a several-year lapse in my membership, I rejoin Costco strictly for their awesome printing deals. Unlike my cousin who once shelled out 800 bucks on her son's bar mitzvah invitations, I can—for the cheapo price of 60 dollars total—procure a heap of two-sided, full-color graduation cards/party invites, with preprinted envelopes tossed in for no extra charge. Who could resist?

The process seems simple enough. Log on to the megastore's website, pick out a prefab design and some colors (I go with purple and gray as background, because Celia's room has been painted lilac since her babyhood. And grey because why not?), add the text, drag photos into the dotted outlines labeled *Place picture here*. Easy peasy.

I offer Celia the option to design (such design as there is) the card with me, but she declines.

"Nuh uh. I trust you," she says. "Really, you got this." Okay.

For the front of the card, I chose Celia's high school graduation pic (of course)—an up-close of my girl: her 500 pounds of mermaid hair surging like the morning tide. With her cheekbones (from me), her almond-shaped (Steven's), lake-blue (mine) eyes. Those lashes sweeping like Chinese fans. Skin clear, strong brows. Her smile like a red ribbon, like she knows secrets, but hell if she's gonna tell. Her nose ring, because what can you do?

The whole of it perfect. Sublime, even.

I drag another graduation photo into the dotted box beside the first. It's pre-school this time. Celia little, round as a bug, similarly sublime. Celi pink, in rose jumper and flushed cheeks. In the lavender graduation hat with its flat top, made earlier that day from construction paper and stapled into shape. Its sides bright with Celi's drawings, a procession of figures—bubble heads, bubble middles, stick stick stick stick for arms and legs. The scrawl of hair. Bellybuttons all around.

I glance at my finished product, the side-by-side photos. I check the dates and address for typos, then check them once more, because you can't be too safe. I click the **Order *Now*** tab. One more errand crossed off my list.

They arrive on a Saturday a couple weeks later, on a rare-for-Detroit sunny afternoon in March, the box sized just so to contain the well-packed stacks of cards and envelopes within.

"Sometimes it pays to go to the big guys," I say to Steven when I nab the package off our porch, note its neatly printed address label, the single strip of tape down the center—no waste, no fuss. "They've really got this thing down."

"Thing?" asks Steven, his voice muffled against the glass of his enormous fish tank, which he's currently cleaning. Or maybe he's just staring into it, counting the occupants to see who's died this week, who's maimed whom, who's on their last fins, and so on.

"You know. The sell-it-cheap, print-it-in-bulk and ship-it-out-lickety-split thing."

"Oh, that thing." But Steven's not paying attention, too caught up in his fishy landscape. He pulls up his sleeve, reaches a long arm into the tank and rearranges the miniature pagoda, shifts the palm tree an inch to the left, rights the dinosaur that's been tipping progressively closer to the rocky floor. Everyone left alive scuttles out of his way, then drifts back soon enough, hoping for lunch.

I stand there for a moment with my newly arrived package, but Steven's clearly hypnotized by this singular world he can control, so I wander upstairs with it tucked beneath my arm.

"Look what's arrived," I say to Celia from the open doorway of her bedroom, that great explosion of clothes, papers, fallen posters, CDs, ancient, but still relevant, plush toys, lipstick tubes and compacts and hair ties strewn like beetles across the wooden floor—what's visible of it, anyway. There are school books, shoes and boots in every color of the rainbow. Two suitcases from a trip we took last year, cat-Lucy snoring inside the open one. The clean, flowery sheets, neatly folded, that still wait on Celia's dresser where I left them two weeks ago—hint obviously untaken. At the window, cat-Aashina clings to Celi's stuffed-full bookcase, gnawing on the curtains with wet, chomping sounds, but an ear-budded Celia couldn't care less as she reclines in the center of her bed-nest, dog-Donna half slumped over her legs.

Celia's my one and only. She's a wonderful kid, sensitive as a coalmine canary, born with an artist's heart and the deep soul-ache that comes from living a thousand lifetimes before this one. She's not much of a housekeeper, though. But it's her space, so who am I to fuss? And after all, she, Steven and I have made the best sort of team for 17-plus years.

"Celi?" I call when she doesn't look up, ensconced as she is among her blankets and heap of dirty sheets, with her old dog and her phone, with whatever texts are zipping back and forth between her and (probably) Archer, the boy she recently started dating. I watch for a moment as her well-bitten thumbs poke poke poke over the little keyboard.

"How can you see through all that?" I ask when she finally notices me, pulls out her ear buds, even as Los Compesinos! goes on moaning through the wires.

"What?"

"All those cracks on your screen. They look worse today."

"Yeah. I might have dropped the phone again."

"Do you want me to take it, get it fixed?"

No!" She's aghast. "I'd be without it for a whole day. Maybe night, too." She closes her eyes, the thought too terrible to bear.

"I can call, see if our guy will do it quicker."

"The one that's always getting stoned in his back office?"

"Yeah. We could go shopping while we waited. There's a great thrift store nearby."

"Eh," says Celia. Unlike me and the rest of my family, Celia's not much of a shopper, and she definitely didn't inherit the bargain gene, that blood-deep desire to pluck treasure from the muck. And the primal satisfaction that comes after a good find. Like a gaping chasm has been filled. For now.

Celia sees my disappointment. "Well, okay. Sure. Maybe next weekend." She puts down the phone, massages her thumbs, first one, then the other. "What do you have there?"

"The invites for your party. The ones I ordered a few weeks ago."

"Oooh, let me see." We take turns with our barely-there nails picking at the single strip of tape across the top of the box. No luck. Finally, Celia grabs a pen, stabs the tip through the box's seam, and it pops, a satisfying sound. From there, the package splits wide, and we fold back the cardboard. Celia picks up the sealed invitations, goes to pull off the plastic covering, then shrugs and bites through it with her sharp little teeth. She pulls out one of the cards, confirms the party date, the directions to our house and so on. She turns it over, studies the two pictures of her taken over twelve years apart.

"Hmmm," she says. Then, "Yeah. Everything looks good." She hands it to me.

I glance down at the photos, Celi small. And Celia as the girl she is right now, just weeks away from graduating high school, mere months from leaving for college. C-Day. "Your *Colossal* day!" I say to her sometimes.

Collapse Day, Calamity Day, Craptastic Day, I repeat in my head, when everything as I've known it for a lifetime—Celia's lifetime—will transform into something new, something arguably tidier, but emptier, starker for sure.

As it's meant to happen. Because children grow up, they leave their first homes and move into their own lives—the alternative being too terrible to bear.

This is the deal I made at Celia's birth: let my Celia survive, I begged whichever deity happened to be floating by. Let her thrive. And when the time comes, I'll let her go.

So I remind myself at night. In the dark, when I can't sleep. When Steven turns over and takes all the sheets with him, then settles again. When Donna moans low through the veil of her doggie dreams, and the rotating fan catches on its hinge and sticks in place, makes a *tick tick tick* that reminds me of time passing, of bargains come to fruition and payments due.

Right now, on this sun-thick afternoon in the deconstructed bedroom, three Celia's look out into the world, one from the center of the forever-unmade bed, two on the card flat in my hand. I run my fingers over the moon-faced youngest, her hand-decorated grad cap with the yarn dangling over one side. The intense focus on her face as she stares outside the photo's edge, toward the picture of her future self. As though, even at five-years-old, she was already plotting to become that very girl.

Real-life Celia gives me her cryptic smile then, and I lie to myself that—like when she was little—we have no secrets between us.

"Love you, Mom," she says, and returns to texting with Archer.

I go downstairs with the box of terrifically priced invitations, which I put down on the antique radio table, the one I picked up last year from somebody's yard sale (only five bucks!). Without bothering to explain, I peel Steven away from his fishes, wrap his arms one at a time around me, and breathe into his shoulder, steadying myself for changes that need—of course, they need—to come.

ROBERT CARR
AIR POCKET

Two hours since I rang the dinner
bell and called across the lake.
I'm sure the boys are at a friend's

house. Oblivious. I carry a birch
branch torch, tight-wrapped
in an outgrown shirt, kerosene

(cont)

flame in my thick-gloved
hand. Muffled pops underfoot, thick
glass, standing hairs, light on ice.

Oak leaves cartwheel on a solid
crust far from green lawns
and swinging sons. I follow

the random spin of leaves and find
a healed bullet wound in the solid
surface. Refrozen out of scale,

time slows in cold. I slide a foot
across the bubbled black hole.
Assault of a fisherman's auger,

the remains of clockwise turning.
I suppress air pocket thoughts.
Fear–the unimaginable upturned face.

Carr

SMALL HOOKED THINGS

Mama teaches
crochet. A ball of shiny
polyester string.

We are making
tea cups on saucers,
soft until soaked
in corn starch.

They harden
like her hair,
A perfect Aqua Net.

(cont)

My breath
is wrapped
in her big
knit sweater,

I love my row
of china, hanging
little handles
on a tree.

I'm smelling
her flaky crust,
pie she cuts
in quarters,

so you never
have to ask
for a second slice.

Carr

FAYE REDDECLIFF
SUPERMARKET SATURDAY

In my red coat, all wool, with money in my pocket, I go to the supermarket. A Saturday outing.

Outside, taped to the plate glass window, hand-printed signs advertise specials on pork chops; below, on the dirty cement, a ragged woman sits mumbling obscenities at my feet. "Fucking bitch," she whispers.

I eat. That is true. Yes. Not well, not a lot, but I eat.

Inside, I walk down aisles of bins and rows that blur with colors and shapes. People browse and look away from loaded shelves to glance at one another.

I choose with care a bright blue package here, a sleek steel can, a shapely yellow container and note how right they look in my grocery cart–a smart, bright collection.

Attracted by red, ripe apples, 89 cents a pound, I wait while a thin, young man in mismatched pants and jacket bends over the bin. While I watch, I'm sure, I think, a tear slides on the waxed red skins.

Get hold of yourself, I say to myself, and hurry away leaving the apples to the man and an Indian family of four.

At the bread counter ("Give us this day our daily . . . ") I encounter a wizened old woman, who leans on her empty cart and asks: "Which do you think is best?"

I advise Whole Wheat Honey Nugget (good for you and tasty, too) even though, I know she asks everyone. It is a conversation gambit, a way to begin a relationship, an exchange, an unlonely moment. Try the parks, try the streets, and when the muggings get too bad, when you fear the night, when you can't stand the hatred, try the wine.

Behind the waist-high counter no one can see Lisa's (the checker) white socks and sensible oxfords. They see instead the stiff-starched pale green uniform that slopes over her breasts, creases at her waist and begins the out and down—not all the way to varicose veins.

Lisa, do you dream of a TV dinner, a deep soft couch and quiet?

When my turn comes, I return Lisa's smile and check her out against the handwritten list taped to the cash register: 1) smile—check; 2) greet customer—check; 3) call prices—check.

With quick, firm movements, she packs—cans on the bottom, crushable and breakable items on top.

I want to put my life on the counter so her capable fingers will sort and order it for me, but I pick up the bag of manageable groceries and leave.

PAULA GOLDMAN
OVERCOAT AS SYMBOL

Freud writes that in women's dreams
an overcoat is a symbol for a man....

I want a man as sleek
as my black shiny rain
slicker, warm as my goose
down parka, dangerous
as my camouflage jacket,

(cont)

durable as my black sheep-
skin. I want him outrageous
and funny, so long as he
doesn't run out of money,
I want him wearing
a faux leopard cape
to the ball. Let him be
true as my old navy pea-
coat, spiffy as my Lord
Chesterfield with its velvet
collar and silver signet
buttons. I want someone
to whom I can holler
down the street, who'll come
running to me, slender
and fluent as my Italian
gabardine, understanding
as a husband can be,
flattering as my gray ultra-
suede, easy to take off
the hanger and go anyplace,
ever see such a man? Stroke him
gently and call this number:
1-800—THE COAT.

Goldman

DOLLY REYNOLDS
LO, HOW A ROSE

    The year that Frances turned ten, it snowed on Christmas Eve. It was 1975 and the winter had been harsh in the small town in New Hampshire. Frances, though, loved every flake that drifted down lazily from the darkening sky. She was trying to finish up the chores at the barn so Joan, the owner of the stables, could make it to her evening Mass, buckling the ponies into their rugs and throwing extra hay down in their stalls. Joan's strong fingers ached in the cold, Frances knew; her teacher was so grateful on nights like this to stay by the woodstove in the tack room with her dogs, talking to parents and finishing up the accounts.

Frances spent every day at the barn. It was just down the hill from her house, and she helped Joan before and after school, cleaning, mucking, feeding, and riding. In the afternoons she stood at Joan's broad hip, helping the small pupils with their mounts, holding up hooves and tightening girths. On cold nights Joan gave all her horses a warm mash, and it was Frances's job to prepare it on Joan's black stove. Frances took special care this Christmas Eve, serving it to the lesson ponies as if they were the Queen's royal mounts, watching the steam rise from the buckets as the ponies plunged their muzzles into the mash, and the smell of the hot bran and molasses mingled with the heady scents of hay and shavings and warm, dusty pony coat and everything that Frances loved in this world. Before Joan left for Mass, she gave Frances her Christmas gift, a small, silver locket with a rose filigreed on the front.

"You are my rose," Joan said quietly, pressing the locket into Frances's hand.

Earlier that day Frances had watched her mother, Elsie, dress for dinner. Her father was coming home and it was Christmas Eve; she could see that her mother was taking special care. Elsie had washed her hair that morning, set it, and let it dry for hours under her bouffant cap. Elsie pulled out her lacy bra and garters, and sprayed perfume, L'Air du Temps, between her small breasts and at the back of her knees. Frances helped to zip her into a white dress and find her dangly jade earrings. Her mother was the most beautiful woman she had ever seen. Other people said so too, all the time, looking at Frances's lumpen figure with quiet surprise.

Frances had a little sister too, Janie, who was seven that year, slim and golden-haired. Janie loved horses too, but she loved model horses. She played with them in her room, dressing them in doll clothes and applying Magic Marker lipstick to their plastic mouths. Next to her sister, Frances knew she was shy and much too plump, lumbering off to school with hay in her hair while her little sister turned cartwheels on the sidewalk in front of her, counting the hours until she could stand with Joan and her ponies in that loamy, rich world that was, to her then, all in all.

Janie had been in her room when Frances had left for the barn earlier that afternoon, forcing doll clothes onto her model horses, choosing the perfect outfits for Misty of Chincoteague and Clydesdale Mare and Foal. Janie kept all her doll clothes in a little red trunk. At the bottom of this trunk, under all the little skirts, pink pajamas, and mini knitted caps, Janie also kept a bottle of vodka that she had taken from their parents' liquor cabinet downstairs. It was a secret. Her parents wouldn't notice one missing bottle, which had now lain in Janie's little trunk for a week. That Christmas Eve Frances had watched Janie open the bottle and take several little sips. Frances hated the taste and the smell of alcohol and didn't see how Janie could keep swallowing it the way she did. She could smell the vodka from where she was sitting, a sharp smell, like a poison arrow in her nose. Her little sister was giggling when Frances left to help Joan.

Frances was the first to hear her father, Neal's, Volkswagen pull into the driveway after she made her way home from the barn.

"Hi, Dad," Frances said at the front door, blocking his entrance with her body as he tried to push past her with his briefcase. When Frances was little, she and her father had always been the first ones awake, Frances, in her rumpled nightgown, curled in a chair in the den with her book and her cat, and Neal shaving in the downstairs bathroom so as not to wake Elsie. There were separate spigots for hot and cold, so Neal had to fill the basin with hot water, which caused the mirror to steam up. When she was little, Frances would sit on the toilet seat and watch Neal as he lathered his cheeks, pretending to be Santa Claus, ho-ho-hoing and asking Frances if she had been a good girl. Those days were long gone, a faded postcard from a foreign country.

"You have something on your face," Neal said as he pushed past her. It was a smear of her Christmas Eve bran mash.

And then, from upstairs, Elsie screamed. And screamed again. And then she screamed for help.

When Frances thinks back to this night, she cannot remember exactly what happened next. She remembers her father shaking Janie and barking at her, "This is not a joke!" There was the ambulance, its lights flashing against the garlands in the hall. She remembers her sister's impossibly small body limp and white on the stretcher, moaning softly with brown vomit caking her golden hair and running down her neck. Frances felt that prick against her nose, that poison arrow, as Janie rolled out past her. Frances was the only one who remembered Janie's parka and her small red boots.

They followed the ambulance to the hospital. Frances sat in the back seat of their station wagon, shivering. She had forgotten her coat.

"They asked me how many of these she had had," her mother said quietly to her father. "I said, how many of what? Fits? Convulsions?"

Elsie took a sip from the Tab can in the cup holder on the door. Frances knew that Elsie often filled these Tab cans with wine to sip while she was driving. It kept her calm, her mother had explained. Neal stared straight ahead, teeth clenched, silent, a slow and careful driver even under these circumstances. He had taught Frances never, ever to let the gas tank get below half full. You never know when you'll have to leave in a hurry.

"Her vomit had that funny smell," Elsie whispered to Neal. "You don't suppose there's any chance—she's just drunk?"

***

Jim Verras was waiting for them in the emergency room. Dr. Jim Verras, the hospital's chief neurosurgeon. Jim had been Neal's roommate all four undergrad years at Yale. They had been close in college, very close, and had settled near each other at the start of their adult lives. Jim had two boys close in age to Frances and Janie, but his wife was also a doctor, short and stumpy, an oncologist of all things, and detested by Elsie. The families had tried to socialize with each other but it was impossible. Elsie told Frances that Jim's wife smelled like the poison chemicals she worked with all day long.

Janie was brought in by the paramedics on a stretcher, two bags of fluids hung from the pole by her head, slim, plastic tubes laced into Janie's tiny arm. Frances saw how grateful her father was to know Jim. Neal wasn't rich like the other boys at his college, Frances knew. His father ran a scrap metal yard outside of New Haven, and Neal had won a scholarship, eating a can of tomato soup for dinner every night to save money. Now Neal was a lawyer and friends with this important doctor who would save Janie's life.

"The world is all before you," Neal had said to Frances once. "Look at me—anything is possible."

Jim had his arm around Elsie's shoulders and was helping to push Janie's stretcher to a treatment area behind the curtain. Neal followed quickly. So quickly that no one noticed Frances standing alone in the emergency room entrance, snow blown in about her feet from the cold night outside.

Jim held a penlight to Janie's eyes and warmed his stethoscope in his hands before listening, carefully, to her heart. Janie was awake now and murmuring. Neal was standing so close to Jim, and Frances could see that her father's cheeks were flushed. Jim had strong hands, Frances saw, with pink, clean nails and black hairs that crisscrossed the backs of his fingers.

Jim was smiling now. Janie's eyes were open and now her lips as well. She said one word: "Thirsty." Now the nurses smiled too. Jim placed his warm hand on Neal's shoulder and told him, "She's going to be okay."

***

Back in the waiting room, a man in a Santa suit sat next to a small Christmas tree. His beard had slipped beneath his chin, and he held a picture book about trains in his lap. He was crying, Frances could see. There was no one else there. Frances stood by the open door, shivering. The man walked up to Frances and took her chubby hand in his.

"You are a nice big girl," the man whispered. "So pretty."

Frances was shaking. You should never be rude to a grown-up, she knew, especially one who is saying nice things.

"You are shivering," the man said to her. "Are you sick?" His breath smelled sweet, like peppermint. Frances shook her head.

"Well then," the man told her, pulling a stethoscope from beneath his coat and lifting her hand to his hip, "you'd better come with me. I might look like Santa but I'm really a doctor. You are big enough to know that Santa is only make-believe." He had put his hands gently on her shoulders and pushed her through the emergency room, careful to make sure she did not slip on the linoleum floor. Her barn boots made sloshing noises with each step.

"We need to get you some dry clothes," Doctor whispered. "We don't want such a pretty girl," the man whispered, rubbing his chin against her cheek, "to catch a chill."

Frances thought about Lynn back at the barn, of the ponies, of the steaming mash she had prepared for them tonight. Had she fed them? Was it burning on the stove? She thought about Jesus, about how he had been born in a manger and how all the animals bowed down and how softly the cow had been lowing.

"Please," she prayed silently to them, the donkey and the lamb, the gentle cow and the baby in his manger. "Please, if it is possible, please take this man away from me."

***

Beyond the double doors there was a corridor, half lit and quiet. It was hard to see. Doctor led Frances to a small room at the end, the darkest room of all. Frances could barely make out a hospital bed, some cupboards, and a sink. Doctor picked her up and laid her on the bed. He was strong.

***

"*What child is this who laid to rest…*"

Doctor was singing, his voice soft and low. Frances lay in the middle of the hospital bed, her feet bare. Doctor had pulled off her wet boots and was drying her feet with a rough, white towel he pulled from the cabinet above the sink.

"*On Mary's lap is sleeping.*"

He opened a drawer by the sink and took out a pair of rubber-soled socks sealed in plastic. A pale shaft of light streamed into the room through a small window in the door to the corridor.

"Whom angels greet, with anthems sweet…"

Frances could make out a web of silver strands, like chicken wire, inside the glass of the window.

"While shepherds watch are keeping."

Doctor took the socks out of the plastic and stretched one over his fingers. His nails were sharp, Frances knew, and his knuckles smelled of soap. He opened his lips, blew deeply into one sock and then pulled it onto Frances's bare foot. The sock was hot and moist from his breath. Doctor did the same thing with the second sock, then folded up the plastic and put it in his back pocket.

"I just need to listen to your heart," he said to her. "Close your eyes."

Once, Lynn's Appaloosa pony had almost died of strangles, abscesses closing off his throat and making it nearly impossible to swallow. Night after night Frances had snuck out of bed and lain with the sick pony on the straw, spooning cider down his hot, swollen throat one teaspoon at a time. To pass those dark hours, Frances would tell the pony stories she remembered reading that day, about Horton the elephant and Yertle the turtle. She counted the spots on his appy rump and the whiskers on his chin and prayed as hard as she could that the pony would one day raise his head again, that he would live.

She didn't exactly pray on that hospital bed with Doctor, but she did remember the sorrel spots splattered across that round, white rump. She remembered the sound of the first ragged nicker that rumbled from his throat. She thought for a minute she heard it again. Doctor had placed his cold, trembling hands on her skin inside her sweater, then inside her panties, and then he left her alone on the bed, closing the door behind him.

Against all odds, the pony had lived. And although she didn't know it then, so would Frances.

***

It was Jim who found her first, sitting in a chair in the emergency room, wrapped up in a hospital blanket with hospital socks on her feet. Her teeth were chattering.

"Frances," Jim whispered, kneeling down, "Janie is going to be okay. We're just keeping her overnight. Your mother is going to stay with her. But she's okay. She's better now. Don't be scared, sweetheart. She's just fine. She just drank something by mistake. She didn't know it wasn't good for little girls to drink."

And then Jim did an amazing thing that Frances would remember all her life. He wrapped his arms around her body and hugged her. He didn't move his arms until she stopped shaking, until she felt her lungs take in air and her heart thud against her chest wall.

Neal, too, was watching, Frances saw, his face exhausted and his chest collapsed. Elsie had to spend the night in the hospital with Janie, he told Frances. He didn't notice she had no shoes until they had made their way across the icy parking lot to the car.

On the drive home from the hospital, Neal had Frances lie across the front seat, close to heater on the dashboard, which he ran at full blast. Frances's head was on the seat close to his lap, and he stroked her hair with his trembling hand while Frances clutched Joan's locket in her hands. On the radio King's Choir, little boys who sounded like girls, was singing "Lo, How a Rose E're Blooming."

"This is Joan's favorite hymn," Frances whispered, her throat ragged.

"Mine too," her father whispered back and sang along softly to his daughter while she trembled in the dark.

ANITA PINATTI
IN PRAISE OF CHARLIE

The blue waters of the Danube dividing
Budapest are flowing far behind us.
A brown emptiness surrounds our bus
waiting too long at "checkpoint Charlie."

A border guard slowly walks the aisle
of our bus with a real gun harnessed
to his shoulder and a face like stone.
We clench our teeth, guard our tongues.
Our baggage on the road is randomly
opened, exposing our pajamas and
toothbrushes, our confusion and
humiliation to the light of day. When
Charlie's bag is opened, several bottles
of vodka glisten in the sun. That's all
it takes to send us on our naïve way.

(cont)

I am still shivering inside a terry robe
beside a thermal bath in Baden,
thinking of that stone-faced boy who
did not look old enough to drink.

A glass of brandy stops my shivers.
Another glass removes the chill.

Pinatti

STEVE COUGHLIN
WAITING ROOM

In the dream he wants his mother to be in the chair beside him. He wants both of them to be sipping steaming coffee from Styrofoam cups waiting for his mother's name to be called.

His mother who must be 79—her lungs still aching with cancer.

He senses she is overdue for an examination. That it's been years since the doctor pointed to the blossoming tumors on his mother's CT scan results.

It's as if pressing upon the white waiting room walls is a vague recognition he will never again sit beside his mother on the couch.

That they will never again watch the final innings of a Red Sox game.

There's a microwave on the countertop flashing 12:00 o'clock and grey swinging doors across the hallway.

He senses there is something wrong with the grey swinging doors.

He hears a high-pitched wind rushing between the doors' thin slit.

He looks at a vase without flowers. He looks at two windows that stare into a night without parking lot lights, without cars driving the streets beyond.

He knows there are no streets beyond.

And it's cold.

(cont)

So cold it feels as if snow might drift from the fluorescent lights.

So cold, he thinks, that if his mother was beside him she would need to be bundled in a heavy winter jacket. The same winter jacket his mother wore when she drove to the package store for cigarettes at 68.

When she would crack the driver's-side window and let cigarette smoke drift into the winter streets.

Before the doctor assured her surgery was not an option.

Before the doctor suggested they discuss comfort measures.

And now he remembers it's been a decade since he's seen his mother's face. That when walking the hallways at work, when reading a book in the living room, he struggles to recall the sound of his mother's voice.

But even now—ten years later—he desires to see clouds of her breath.

He still wants to look upon the redness of his mother's chapped hands as they wait for a nurse to call her name.

A nurse in green scrubs confirming his mother still has something to hope for.

Even if the microwave continues to flash.

Even if snow collects at the nurse's feet.

Even if the high-pitched wind rushes through the swinging grey doors, which he knows—has always known—is really the sound of nothing.

Coughlin

LIZA WOLFF-FRANCIS
THE SYNCHRONIZATION OF MARRIAGE

It was a smaller office than would be expected for a place that did such things. Things that were now considered important but still had a seedy taste to them. It might as well have been a tanning salon and all that implies. The tile floor was shiny, but the walls were the color of cardboard. And unlike a tanning salon, it was dimly lit and drab, all of it drab. Walls bare, except a couple of taped-up paper signs saying all parties must be present and accounted for and then a list of the needed documents. The line of people waiting was an actual line, like one you might expect at a bank on a Friday afternoon. People shuffled their feet and every few minutes looked around them, then down, in some combination between anxious and bored. There was nowhere to draw a number, though there were five rows of brown metal folding chairs and some people sat while the person they were with waited in line. Everyone refused to make eye contact, as if by not making eye contact they would be invisible. Haley would have easily believed she was in the line alone if it wasn't for Jack breathing behind her like a bulldog.

"Can you breathe a little quieter," Haley asked.

"What?" Jack hadn't been looking at her and his hearing wasn't very good.

"We're getting closer," Haley said, rolling her eyes.

The odd mix of people was not apparent, until you looked at them as couples. There was an eighty-five-year-old man, pants baggy around his shrunken body and held up with a cinched belt. He stood with a twenty-two-year-old blonde in a pink mini skirt. He looked like her grandfather and she laughed like a puppy yelps, but in this office, it was obvious that grandfather-granddaughter was not the relationship. Or how about the thirty-five-year-old teacher and the twenty-year-old athlete who had most assuredly been her student throughout high school, if not middle school? Haley and Jack were just another odd pair.

It was now only one week before her and Jack's procedure and subsequent scheduled wedding at the courthouse. Neither of them would have admitted there was no love between them and they certainly wouldn't have written it on the nosy forms, but their friends and family knew. The couple had only known each other for three weeks. Not that there is a certain amount of time that it takes people to fall in love, but the agenda for love wasn't set. No one expected it, no one hoped for it, and no one really even wanted it. Any one of the people who knew them would have easily said that they weren't in it for love. But not all marriages are for love.

The line shuffled forward. They stepped up to the counter.

"Do you have all your documentation?" the woman asked.

Haley handed over a manila folder with all of the filled-out forms, signed agreements, and notarized certificates, everything that would make this legal and binding.

The woman took all the papers out, signed two of them and scanned them.

Jack gave her a check.

"Now you can go ahead with the procedure. We will scan the rest of the paperwork and have it ready. Just bring these two forms with my signature." The woman handed them the forms and peered back at the computer. "It looks like you are scheduled for one week today at 2:00 pm."

Five hours later, Haley stood in her room looking at her suitcase, waiting for her younger sister to come over. She would stay at Jack's house for the week.

"To be rich and successful, first you must act rich and successful and believe you already are," Haley told her sister numerous times. She thought of this as she went to answer the door.

She and her sister sat on the white leather sofa in her apartment drinking martinis because Haley said martinis are what the rich and famous people drink.

"You know the Evenly Distributed Years Act?"

"The Gold Digger gig?" her sister laughed, but when Haley didn't laugh with her, she quickly added, "The Age-O-Status thing, right?"

"Yeah. The one to alter ages if there is an age difference of more than seven years, to be in compliance with the law."

"Whatever. It's one of the most insane things I've ever heard of." Her sister flipped her hair back. "I mean, we're not just talking about re-writing a couple of numbers on a birth certificate, it's altering a person to be physically older or younger inside and out. Changing someone's age, body, and identity. Kind of like playing God."

"I'm going to do it."

"What? Really? You are going to be an old lady. From one day to the next."

"Not that old. I'll be forty-four." Haley tapped her fingernails against the glass, watching the martini wobble inside. "And rich."

"Forty-four! You're twenty-five. That's a huge leap."

"Look at me. I have major debt and I work as a receptionist for a law firm I hate. The main lawyer guy has a picture of his face, acne and all, with his finger pointing out at you from billboards on the side of the expressway. That should tell me something."

"Yeah, that he's a freak," her sister laughed. "Holy crap, you're not marrying that guy, are you?"

"Ew no. It's Mike's dad. Mr. Ponce. Jack."

"Mike's dad? Interesting."

Haley met Mike in college. They used to smoke pot together and sit in Mike's dorm room talking about sixties music versus today's pop songs. He wore his brown hair in a ponytail and always wore jeans and a t-shirt. It was a somewhat disheveled look Haley was attracted to. She liked him. Some of her friends said even though he wasn't that nice, she would do anything for him. Haley swore to her sister she was marrying Mike's dad for the money, not to get closer to Mike. That would just be weird.

Mike's mother and father had been older parents and they got divorced when Mike was a child. His mother never let Mike spend time with his dad because her relationship with him was so difficult. Instead of fight it out in the courts, Jack left and never saw his son. When Mike's mother died a few years back, his father was the only family he had left. Mike had gotten to know him better since he turned eighteen and now even more since his mother's death. He didn't ask Haley to marry his father, he just mentioned one day when they were hanging out that he and his father were going to try to hire someone to get the procedure done with his father and then marry him.

"I don't want to lose any time with him, Mike said.

"How much will you pay this person?" Haley asked.

"A million dollars."

She was interested. They talked more about it and she said she would do it. It would help Mike and his father and would help her financially. Win. Win. Win.

"And they're paying me," she said to her sister.

"Oh, okay. So, it's all about the money?"

"Obviously. In one week, we will have the procedure. In two, we will be married and they will pay me one million dollars. I will be a millionaire. Plus, I can get the procedure again some day if I want to be younger again. Meanwhile, I will pay off my loans, buy a house, and get that car."

"The Mustang."

"Yeah, the red convertible one."

"Well, *that* is awesome. But why do you have to go so old?"

"Forty-four isn't that old. Jack is sixty-three. There is a thirty-eight-year difference between us. It is against law to marry someone more than seven years older, right? So, thirty-eight divided in half is nineteen. Each of us either adds or subtracts nineteen years from our lives. We end up the same age."

"Forty-four."

"Right. And I will be rich." Haley stood up. "I have to pee," she announced.

Past the walls she had painted deep wine maroon, the framed Escher poster, into the small bathroom. The next day she would go stay with Jack and if things went well, move into his house, where there were bigger bathrooms and chandeliers and everything would be modern and pretty. And if she didn't stay with Jack forever, one day she would buy her own house. Guys would be so impressed, so would her girlfriends, who she would have because everyone would want to be friends with her. A million dollars is a lot. Sure, there are people doing it for two million or so, but this was the deal that came up for her. Plus, the older you are, the more the rate goes down. The procedure and the whole shebang would change things up, add a little excitement to her life.

In the bathroom, she stared in the mirror. She was pretty, even if she said so herself. She had just gotten a new spray tan and it made her look like the Los Angeles sun had loved her. She liked to go topless at the Moorea beach club where she was complemented on her perfect tan and skin and body. She wondered if she would still go tan there in her new body. She tried to squint wrinkles into her face, make lines in her forehead. How would she look at forty-four? She wondered if she was ready for this change. Would she be smarter? What would it be like to age overnight? What if she couldn't handle it? She let her face relax into itself again. She looked into her eyes, tried to somehow see the answers to all her questions in them. She stared back with doe eyes. The skin around them, fresh still, ready for life, for adventure, for something new.

"I'm twenty-five. Forty-four isn't that old. I'll still be fucking hot," she mumbled to herself before she left the bathroom.

Back in the living room, her sister had her shoes off and her feet up on the couch.

"Don't forget we are being sophisticated."

Her sister put her feet down but rolled her eyes. "Wasn't there that 'Right to Age' movement that said once you were an adult, you should be able to make your own choices about who to marry?"

"Yeah, but it only stuck around for about a month. Then Age-O-Status came in with their scientific breakthrough."

"Why don't you wait a year, make sure you still feel the same way. Don't rush it."

"Unfortunately, there is kind of a rush. When both people agree to the procedure, it has to take place when one person in the couple is at a half-decade marker, though it begins at twenty. So, one person has to be at age 20, 25, or 35, or 45, or 55, etc."

"Why? That's a weird rule."

"I guess there's not enough technology to handle it otherwise. It is also supposed to deter couples from having the procedure for alternative reasons."

"Like you have?"

"Yeah."

"So, the machine or whatever just evens out your ages?"

"Right."

"It's literally right out of a sci-fi movie."

Haley laughed. "I know, but it's a lot of money." Her leg shook.

"Do you think you'll consummate?" Haley's sister smiled a sly smile.

"Consummate?" Haley giggled. "That's a weird word."

Her sister burst out laughing. "Do you think you two will have sex?"

"I don't know. It's not part of the contract. Plus, he's old. It's gross."

Her sister held up her glass to toast her. "We should celebrate your upcoming new birthday. Your move into forties." She lifted the bottle up.

"To money," Haley said, crossing her legs and taking a larger swig of her drink than she intended.

Haley had taken off work for the week and she and Jack had decided to spend time together getting to know each other. Jack's house was a one-story large expansive modern box with lots of windows and a blue front door with front yard landscaping that looked like Japanese gardens. As she walked in, the smell of fresh cooked food hit her.

"Come in and have a seat," Jack called to her.

She walked into the kitchen as he pulled roasted potatoes out of the oven. "I've got dinner almost ready."

"Okay, sure," Haley said, not at all sure.

"I used to be a chef."

"So, you know your way around a kitchen."

"Somewhat, at least."

"Well, it smells amazing."

Jack served them each a plate and dimmed the lights in the kitchen just slightly.

"I'm really not trying to set the mood, the light in the kitchen is just bright. I've never been one for bright lights."

"Me either," Haley said. "No worries."

Jack sat down across from her at the table for six. There were fresh flowers in a vase in the center, which he moved to the side to be able to see her better. She hadn't noticed the low playing Simon and Garfunkle in the background until now.

"Bon appetite."

"Yes, bon appetite."

They both began to eat. Haley sat upright chewing every bite fifteen times and touching her napkin to her lips between every bite, putting it back into her lap between bites.

"It's a little weird sitting with me, right?"

"No offense, and not that I would really know, but you kind of seem like a dad."

"I am a dad."

"Of course," Haley laughed. "I know that, but for a minute, I almost forgot."

"Part of this I am doing for my son. I want to have more time with him."

"That's beautiful," Haley said. "I never really had a father. He wasn't in my life."

"I'm sorry. I was that guy too."

Haley's eyes welled up with tears. She had her arms crossed in front of her and pinched the skin over her abdomen to try to keep from crying.

"So, you're doing this all for Mike?"

"Well, no. Part of it is for him. The other part is for me. I want to live longer. The doctor told me a few months ago that I have a heart problem and have about a year to live. He said if I could only go back in time. So, that is what I am doing."

"But making yourself younger isn't going back in time."

"No, but if I am younger, my heart problems won't be there yet and a younger body can sustain more. The doctor was convinced this was the best solution to living longer. He didn't outright advocate for it, because that would be illegal, but said if it were possible, it would be a solution. It's die sooner or later for me. I'm choosing later."

"Wow, so this is really an important procedure."

"Life or death, let's say." Jack laughed and raised his wine glass.

That first night they seemed to connect. When Jack showed her to her room, Haley felt surprised at how tender he seemed, how kind. She hugged him. She definitely didn't want him to die. This would help him. And her.

Haley slept soundly that night. In the morning, they ate omelets and drank coffee on the back porch. They talked about dreams and what it meant to change their ages.

"For me, it's like a second chance at life. More time to live. I'm not ready to die. To be honest, I'm terrified of dying."

Haley rubbed his arm with a gentleness she had previously only held inside. That touch was that moment when Haley felt she was really beginning to care about him.

They swam in his pool and in the afternoon, drove around the mansions of Beverly Hills, talking about all the stars. Jack pointed out the ones he had visited.

"How did you get to go to their houses?"

"I know people from business. It's all about networking in the City of Angels, the stars are in there too."

"Well, I've never met any stars and I've lived here my whole life."

"Those are just the circles I run in," Jack laughed.

Haley giggled. She was impressed. Usually, she prided herself on always being able to contribute something to the conversation, but didn't know what to say.

The third day they drove down to the San Diego zoo, looked at the animals, ate churros, and talked about natural habitats. Jack did animal impressions. His giraffe was perfect. Haley laughed and laughed.

"It's exciting to get to know someone new, someone who will be my wife." Jack smiled at her. "And someone so pretty."

Haley blushed. "It's crazy to think we are going to be married in less than a week," she said. "And that we'll be different ages than we are now."

"You just have to remember, the important thing is staying young in your mind."

Day four, Jack took her to Huntington Harbor where they took his catamaran out.

"You have a sailboat?"

"I learned to sail as a boy, but it's something I started to really love when I got this boat. It is the captain of the Pacific. And the coast is just gorgeous from the ocean."

"I've never been on a sailboat."

"Why don't we go over to Catalina Island. It's five hours or so on the boat, but we can stay the night and come back tomorrow. What do you think?"

"Sure. I've never been there either."

"Well, let's go. Why not?"

Jack handled the boat like a pro. Dolphins rode along beside them for over an hour and the spray of the ocean made Haley feel alive.

In Avalon, Jack got two hotel rooms, one for each of them, they explored the shops and restaurants. Haley wondered how she had never been there before, it was the perfect place for her. For dinner they went in one of the restaurants. The maître d' greeted Jack by name, calling him Mr. Ponce, and took them to a table he referred to as Jack's favorite. When they sat down and drinks were ordered, Haley looked at the menu prices, the white table cloths, the art on the walls, and felt a little intimidated.

"How do you know this place? I mean, how do they know you?"

"Remember how I said I used to be a chef?"

"Well, I wasn't officially a chef. I used to own a restaurant out here and a couple in town. They know me because I know the owner. We used to do business together."

"There is so much I don't know about you."

"There is so much I don't know about you either and there will be plenty of time to learn it all."

Haley started to think about what he didn't know about her. She hadn't done that much, not like him. He didn't know some things, like that her mother taught her to sew, how as a kid she dreamed of being a fashion designer, how she majored in anthropology only because she had the most credits in it, how once she danced at a strip club for one night only and made three hundred dollars. Maybe he didn't have to know everything.

"So, what experience do you have with love?" Jack asked her.

"Not much," she said. "The relationship with my first real boyfriend ended badly. I walked in on him cheating on me with another woman."

"My ex-wife, Mike's mother, walked in on me doing the same thing. Our relationship had gone sour, but I still regret the way it ended. It was totally my fault."

"Oh."

"Awkward. Sorry."

"For me, there was a whole blow-up scene. I chased her out of the house while my boyfriend shielded her with a towel, telling me to 'calm down.'"

"That sounds familiar. Many years ago. But familiar."

"Taking a break from the dating scene will be good for me."

"A break? Who knows if we get along, right?"

"We seem to. I just meant...."

"What if we don't like each other's looks after it's all done?"

"I can see how you were cute, I mean, you are a handsome man. I doubt...." Haley stumbled over her words. She didn't want to say he had probably been good looking but now wasn't because he was old, but that is exactly what she meant and it was obvious.

"Well, we don't have to worry about you. You're gorgeous, that won't change."

Again, Haley blushed.

Clearly, Jack had a lot of money. She thought about her sister's comment about the gold digger gig and wondered if that's what she was, a gold digger. She was getting ready to marry this old guy, basically for money. Her life would be so much easier, and despite some of the things he had done, he was cool. And she was helping him. And Mike. But mostly him; she was keeping him from dying. Really, it was like she was saving his life.

When they got back from Catalina Island, they walked down to Huntington beach and ate oysters and french fries. The wind was soft. People on bicycles roared by on the path. The sand was cool on her feet. She took his hand, steadied him on the sand.

"You've told me you are doing this to pay off your loans and meet some of your financial goals, but how is it for you to be making such a huge, amazing leap?"

"I know I'm going the other direction with my age, but there is a part of me that also feels like I am getting another chance, but a totally different one, a unique one, one that brings a whole new adventure that I am ready for."

"Good. I think I'm ready for it too. Nervous, but ready."

Haley giggled. "Yes, nervous. Definitely."

"Somehow, the best things in life make you nervous."

"Twenties haven't been all that and I doubt thirties are that great. I don't think I'm really missing much. I'm excited for what is to come."

What Haley had not expected was that she began to feel an

affection for Jack that felt like love. Love seemed like a strong word and she had too much to lose to call it that. What if he talked her out of the money or tried to change the arrangement? They had documents drawn up, but these cases rarely held up in court.

The night before the procedure, Jack and Haley went to see the musical *Jersey Boys*. She wore the dress she wore to homecoming her senior year, which amazingly, she still had, and, luckily, still fit. She put on her lipstick and checked out her body as much as she could in the bathroom mirror. She was excited about her time with him and didn't care if anyone wondered if they were a couple or father and daughter.

Afterwards they went for coffee and dessert.

"It's late for an old fogey like me, but I'll be up for even more after the procedure. We can go out, experience the ever-changing world."

"I don't think I realized how much I enjoy going to the theater."

"You are just discovering the world. I can't wait to do forties again, with you."

That was when he kissed her and she kissed him back. Haley was surprised to feel butterflies in her stomach, that she was smiling inside and nothing about her was grossed out. His face stubble was coarser than most of the guys she made out with, but the kiss felt magical like she thought a first kiss should.

That night she slept beside him, they curled into each other, held each other, felt each other's bodies, knowing they would change.

On the day of the procedure, Haley felt good about it. The papers they signed said they would get married within a week or reimburse the state one million dollars. Legally, they were ready. Again, they waited in the mundane line of anxious people surrounded by empty cardboard-colored walls.

All of the paperwork was fully processed. This time, they were called to the other side of the building. The procedure was completed in two and a half hours. When they were released, they were exhausted. They looked each other up and down and mumbled quick compliments back and forth about how they turned out.

The procedure wasn't invasive in the same way surgery is, but it was an exhausting one for the body since so many different parts were being aged or un-aged, as the case may be. They went back to Jack's house to lie down. Each thought the other looked pretty good. Though, in the bathroom, Haley stared into the mirror waiting to recognize herself again.

Much of her brown hair was gray and she had those spider web wrinkles at the corners of her eyes. Even her hands looked older. She aged nineteen years in a couple of hours; it would take some getting used to. Jack had already seen himself at this age. For him, it was a matter of memory retrieval. For her, it was an imagining of who she was now.

Early evening around 6:30, phone messages from his family, from her sister, were building up. Mike called his father several times, but it was all Jack could do to say they had the procedures done and were going to sleep. Haley sent her sister a quick message saying all was good and she'd call later. They slept until seven the next morning when Jack got up to go to the bathroom. Haley opened her eyes to look at him briefly before closing them again. She heard him shuffle to the bathroom, pee and then there was a scratching and wheezing noise that woke her from the dozing state she was still in.

"Are you alright?" she called out to him.

When he didn't answer directly, she got out of bed, and pushed her way into the bathroom. In his cotton white boxers and undershirt, Jack was hunched over, clutching his chest. Haley shrieked and ran for her cell phone. She called 911, ran to unlock the front door for the paramedics, then back to the bathroom. She hoped she would find him laughing at her for falling for his horrible joke, but instead, he had slumped to the floor, pulling the towel rack with the maroon towels down with him. The towels covered him and somehow in her imagination, they looked like blood.

"Hold on," she told him. "We're in this together now."

"I guess it's going to be sooner," he said from the floor.

"No. You're still here. I love you. Stay with me."

He was getting paler and paler. She saw life leaving him. She pushed his body flat on the ground and gave him mouth to mouth the best she could from a mandatory class she took for work the year before.

Her palms were sweaty on his arms. She breathed into his mouth. She pumped his chest. Finally, the E.M.T.s arrived, used the defibrillator, then whisked him away to the hospital. In her pajamas, with her hazards on, she followed right behind the ambulance, praying for him to be okay. She felt like she couldn't breathe. Jack was dead on arrival.

When Mike arrived, he cried like Haley had never seen a man cry. They held each other there at the hospital and then again at Jack's house. Mike told her he hadn't recognized her at first with her new look. Haley still felt like her old self, though she ached and was unsure if it was the procedure, her age, or the circumstances. It was all so new and unbelievable.

That day, Haley's sister invited her to coffee. Haley didn't say anything over the phone, but decided to wait to tell her. In the coffee shop, there were very few people and it was a quiet space. Her sister gasped an audible gasp when she saw her.

"You still look hot," she added quickly.

"Jack's gone," Haley told her and started crying.

"What do you mean, gone?"

"He died. We woke up and I heard him in the bathroom."

"What?"

"He had a heart attack."

"That's awful."

"I gave him CPR. I gave him mouth to mouth as he was dying. I tasted death in my mouth," Haley cried more.

"Oh, disgusting…sorry."

"And now he's not here. I can't believe he's gone. It has all been so horrible."

"You're still going to get the money, right?"

"After the funeral is over, I'm sure. But, I don't know what I'll do without him."

"The Mustang. New house. It will still be great. And easier, I mean, you don't have to deal with someone else and being married."

"But, I liked him."

Mike arranged the funeral for three days later. Haley went dressed in black as she imagined a widow would, though she wasn't really the widow. She was no one, except someone who had altered her entire DNA composition for him. That had to be close to love. But it wasn't much of anything official or socially recognizable.

She heard nothing about the contract and the money she was owed. Not wanting to be rude, she didn't bring it up at the funeral. Two more days went by. She didn't want to be insensitive, but she also wanted to go ahead and wrap up the payment details, especially since she still planned on quitting her job and now felt even more inspired to do so. She called Mike, but he didn't answer, and her call went to voicemail. He still hadn't called back after a couple of days, but she knew he was grieving. She called again. And again. Finally, she went looking for him and when she found him at his house, he told her the contract was void because she and Jack hadn't married. He even said he was thinking of asking for the money back that they already paid her, but since she had gone through with the procedure, he would be nice and let her have it. Haley was furious.

"Let me have it? I changed my chronological age for your father. It's not my fault he died. I was going to marry him. You still owe me the money."

"I am mourning my father, which is something you can't understand. I'm not trying to blow you off, Haley, but I'm not up for this conversation. If you read the contract, it clearly states that the money will be transferred when you are married. But you two didn't marry."

"I understand you are grieving, Mike. I am also mourning him and this entire situation, as well as my old self."

"You didn't even care about him, it was all about money for you."

"That's not true. We got to be close in the week before his death. I was falling in love with him. But that doesn't matter. We had a contract and you owe me money."

They argued back and forth. Neither of them budged.

Haley called her lawyer who said he would help her. They scheduled a meeting for the next day. Realizing a week had passed, the lawyer had to file a petition to the state for Haley and Jack to not be married due to the fact one party was now deceased. There was still a charge of ten thousand dollars, half of which Mike would have to pay. Her lawyer called Mike's lawyer and that issue was settled within a few days, but the larger amount that had been agreed on was a tougher battle.

It was about a week and a half before Haley really realized the magnitude of what had happened to her body, she felt the effects of aging years in a couple of hours. Things were different. She had aches and pains that seemed to settle in for the long haul. There was less time for her life now, the end perhaps sooner or later. She had to reevaluate what she wanted and she realized it wasn't what she had thought. And the Moorea beach club seemed far in the past. Not that she couldn't go, she was still a good-looking woman, but she felt more vulnerable, like maybe she shouldn't be there, like maybe no one would want to look at a half-naked old person. It was a thing from a different life.

Weeks dragged on and still Haley saw nothing of the money. Her sister had called at least twenty times but Haley hadn't called her back because of the gasp she made. She didn't want to tell her all about the money and how Mike was being a jerk.

She didn't quit her job and the lawyer with his big face on the billboard, who had never paid attention to her before, said he wasn't sure she was still right for her job. She wondered if it was about her age. She spent mornings covering the new wrinkles on her face as best as she could and nights staring at herself in the mirror trying to figure out who she was now in this new body and trying to imagine what life she missed. Her favorite jeans didn't fit anymore and the buttons on her shirts pulled at the fabric around her stomach and breasts and she constantly noted the way her body felt different at forty-four than it had at twenty-five, how her face looked more sunken, her eyes more tired. She stayed at her apartment with the maroon wine walls and thought about selling the Pier One mirror. The lawyer fees added up, reaching five thousand dollars before she decided to call it quits. The ten thousand they had given her was spent all on righting the situation and it hadn't been fixed.

Haley hadn't felt much older when she first got the procedure, but now she did. This wasn't the way it was supposed to be. She wanted to go back to the boring bank-like line with Jack. Back to the catamaran. To the zoo. To his giraffe impression. To that quick glimpse of love. To another time. She wanted him there with her again. She wanted this to have turned out differently. She had to try to believe she hadn't missed anything, just the years in between then and now.

PATRICIA CANTERBURY
FAVORITE FISHING HOLE

The smells of musky black earth and metallic,
glacier-fed water bring me joy even as I
ache for Joe's voice and gentle kiss. I gather
the folds of my skirt—not black, no sir. Only starbursts
of green, blue and gold. Joe's favorite colors.
I sit on a sun-kissed boulder wedged against the south
bank of languorous Skagit River, alongside a shaded pool
where toothy trout strike innocent minnows. I see Joe's smile,
the one he always wore when one of those trout
latched onto his bait.

(cont)

Tadpoles dart and water bugs skitter
across the pool's indigo surface. I remove the lid
from a silver urn, giant dark firs and friendly pines
watching every move. I say to myself
what's so often said— that we are merely the stuff
of water and dust—only now it seems not just any old dust,
but nothing short of stardust. Can you imagine it?
We humans, meager sparks of life,
mingling with the stars.

Joe took delight in simple things—a good day
of fishing, a plate of fried chicken, a little
TV before bed and always a good-night kiss.
My Joe was just a man, neither saint
nor demon, but he will always
be my very own star.

I stream gray ashes into the pool, grief
bleeding from my hands, stirring dark waters.
The ashes swirl and float, slip downstream, collecting
brown leaves and dying fish. I smooth my skirt
and trek the bank, following Joe to continue our journey
of forty-six years. The river bends and narrows. His ashes
splash onto a dark barren shore. I stop, bite my lip
and grip my skirt. Gray ashes blend into black,
water evaporating and gathering in my heart

Canterbury

CHARLES HALSTED
THE DAWN FREIGHT

Awakened from a sleep-shrouded state
by the distant growl of clickety-clacks, I
recall the sights of capsized grocery carts

(cont)

along the bank of the ditch by the tracks
out of town, the forlorn tents of the homeless
who hover below with nowhere else to sleep,
hear distant deafening blasts from the horn
of the freight. I stagger across the floor, splash
water on my face, move into the kitchen, turn
the kettle on to boil, smell the pungent aromas
of tea from Ceylon. Moving out the front
door, I retrieve today's news from the drive:

"Trump defends tear-gassing children,
ripping babies from mothers' arms,
warns of chaos, injuries, even deaths."

Halsted

BOXED IN

You start to feel the walls closing in when
you take a tumble the second time, let's say
on a sidewalk when you trip on a crack, or
worse when you forget to step up on a curb.

You start to feel the walls closing in
when your mind begins to wander at the
critical time as your car does the same
instead of staying your side of the line.
Perhaps there's a real solution: let
your wife take over the wheel, give up
your freedom, accede to her pleas to move
into your town's retirement home, as
dismal and dreary as it may seem.

Once you've settled in and your life's
no longer your own, restricted to long
dark corridors of impending doom, you'll
know you've come full circle when once
again you begin to drool.

Halsted

SUSAN TRIEMERT
ONLY THE PRETTY ONES

Toward the end of the week, Sally Jo's father called to invite her to his apartment to go swimming. At this point, her parents had been separated for eight months, and even though her dad had moved into his new place several months earlier, Sally Jo hadn't been over. For the first few weeks after he left, he'd crashed at his buddy Dozer's place. Sally Jo didn't know much about Dozer, not even his real name, but she did know that her mother hated the man. "Dozer the Drunk," she'd call him. Nightly, Dozer would phone the house, asking her father to meet him at Shel's, the local bar, to watch the game. Shel's, a few blocks over, was a real "shit-hole," as her mother would say, smelled like armpits and dirty jockstraps. Though Sally Jo wasn't sure how her mother knew what a jockstrap smelled like, especially a dirty one, since the only sports her father played were bowling and darts.

Because the invitation from her father had taken so long, Sally Jo suspected her mother had been behind it. Sally Jo hadn't seen him much since he'd started dating Rosalie, who happened to be the mom of the lead spiker on her seventh grade volleyball team. Sally Jo liked Lucia, Rosalie's daughter, just fine but hadn't spent much time with her outside of practice. So on Saturday when Sally Jo's mother drove her the twenty minutes to his apartment complex, on the outskirts of Apple Valley, Sally Jo couldn't wait to hang out with her dad like they used to, just the two of them.

As her mother pulled into the parking lot, Sally Jo chewed on her cheek and lips, bit at a hangnail, and another. Pulling and stretching, she yanked at the ends of her navy blue gym shorts; she regretted not wearing longer ones, anything to cover more of her skinny chicken legs.

Before getting out of the car, she angled herself up to the rearview mirror to check her braces.

"You look fine, honey." Her mom kissed the top of her head. "Now go have some fun."

Once out of the car, Sally Jo looked around—this was not what she'd expected: several three-story buildings, all painted white, stood guard alongside a tennis court and gated pool area. She couldn't mistake the moist scent of freshly cut grass. The lawn looked ripe and plush, the kind of grass you wanted to dig your toes into, and leave an imprint. Up above, beyond the tips of the evergreens and patches of oak leaves, clouds hung low and loose. As if that wasn't enough beauty to absorb in a single moment, down the pebbled walkway, past the wrought iron gate, water tossed and twinkled in the jade-colored pool.

As her father had instructed, Sally Jo met him near the pool's entrance at 11:00. At first she didn't recognize him; he had on shiny red swim trunks she'd never seen and a baseball cap on backwards. He looked tanner, less hairy, too. From behind his back, he brandished a plain, wide-brimmed sunhat. It looked like the one she'd lost the summer before when they'd been boating.

"Thanks, Dad." She put it on and pulled it tight over her ears. "I didn't know you'd bought that for me."

He shrugged off her remark and told her to follow him to his spot near the whirlpool.

"You believe they've got a Chacuzzi here, Kiddo? Not bad, huh?"

"Jacuzzi, Dad, with a J," she mumbled back, out of earshot.

This pool looked nothing like the public one near her house. Here, tan, blonde-haired girls in neon bikinis filled an entire row of lounge chairs; dry-haired couples sipped their fancy drinks as they sprawled across mattress-sized floaties; and two guys in metallic shades threw a Nerf football in a rainbow-shaped arch. No one was using the pool to swim. There was no lifeguard either, but Sally Jo felt relief knowing that four red inner tubes hung from the wire fence, and one of those long poles with a hooked end—the kind used to yank someone off of a stage—sided up against the kiddie pool. Relieved, too, knowing that this past spring, as a part of her babysitter training, she'd taken (and passed) a CPR course.

Sally Jo lugged her beach bag stuffed with goggles, a snorkel set, her SPF, a paperback, and a change of clothes across the cement. Her dad stopped in front of people. People who looked familiar. Pretty people. There sat Lucia from volleyball and her mom Rosalie. Her father had never mentioned they'd be here. Rosalie said hello while Lucia, in a cute, cherry-red two piece, motioned for Sally Jo to sit next to her on a blanket.

"Nice pool, huh?" said Lucia, as she picked up her stack of Cosmos and scooted over to make room; whenever she shifted, her shiny black hair shook down her back. Sally Jo forced her eyes away, didn't want to get caught staring.

"Yeah. First time here," Sally Jo said as she fanned out her beach towel. Once settled, she smoothed down the split ends of her own dishwater blonde, and regretted that she'd worn the royal blue one-piece that she'd bought for sleep-away camp, not that she had many others to choose from.

"First time here? Really?" Lucia looked confused. "Mom and I've been here twice this week."

"Oh, it's just that I have an issue with chlorine, and my dad wanted me to be cautious," she lied. Before the forming tears could spill, Sally Jo turned away, folded up the edge of her towel and dabbed at the corners of her eyes.

Her father, who hadn't seemed to notice she was upset, walked over and handed her a plastic sack. "Looks like you both have magazines now." He smiled. Inside the bag were the two most current *National Geographic*s. She and her dad liked to research all of the places they hoped to travel to one day. Nepal, the Alps, Papua New Guinea. At home, her bulletin board was covered with photographs of their desired destinations. Sally Jo wanted to read both of these issues cover to cover, but not now, not in front of Lucia. Sally Jo thanked her dad and slid the magazines back into the plastic sack.

Lucia squirted tanning oil into her palm and smeared it onto her arms and legs. Sally Jo couldn't help but notice how long and tan Lucia's legs were, spotless too, and how they glistened and shimmered with the newly applied oil. Eying her own pasty legs, Sally Jo traced the moles and freckles on her thigh, ran her palms up her calves, against the sharp hairs. Against the grain.

Earlier in the week, while playing kickball at the rec center, Sally Jo skidded across the gravel, leaving a pebbled and puckered raspberry on her shin. Now, on the blanket, she picked at the scab, peeling away flecks until blood streamed down to her ankle. Before anyone would notice, she grabbed her beach towel and wiped her leg clean. Leaning back on propped elbows, Lucia had shut her eyes, and even though she wasn't wearing any headphones—and there was no music to be heard elsewhere—she tapped her toes to a steady beat. Only a cool person could pull that off, thought Sally Jo.

It wasn't long before Sally Jo's father and Rosalie had moved onto the same towel and didn't seem to mind how their calves and thighs grazed one another in this sticky heat. When it was humid out, Sally Jo couldn't tolerate having her own limbs make contact, having to peel skin from skin. She grabbed a book out of her bag, a mystery, and flipped through the pages, but kept reading the same paragraph over. Each time she lost her place, she'd glance up to see her father either whispering into Rosalie's ear or rubbing sunscreen onto her upper back. He kept peeling back the straps of her royal blue one piece, a suit that Sally Jo's mom would have liked, though her mother, if she'd been the one wearing it, would've complained about how awful it made her saddle bags, sagging boobs, and gut look.

Sally Jo leaned towards her father. "Wanna hop in with me?"

"Darn, I just put sunscreen on. Maybe in a bit."

Lucia's foot stopped tapping. "What about the chlorine?" she said, without opening her eyes. "I can smell it from here."

"You're probably right." Sally Jo tried to sound chipper. "Best to stay dry."

After some moments passed, her father dug into the cooler and offered her and Lucia each a grape juice box and a tuna fish and tomato sandwich. Sally Jo hadn't had a juice box since she was seven, six years earlier—now that her father was a single parent, maybe he figured he'd better try harder, come prepared and all. It was clear that Rosalie had brought the sandwiches; her father would've made them with roast beef, salami, or ham. That, and these had been tucked into neat little baggies, twisted shut with metal ties. Her father only wrapped food in tinfoil. Wrapped most things in tinfoil, actually: TV antennas to enhance the signal, his collection of matchbooks, various sizes of nails.

With only a few bites left, Sally Jo overheard Lucia asking her mom for some change. Jiggling the coins in her hand, Lucia leaned toward Sally Jo. "They have vending machines in the fitness center next door. Wanna walk over with me?"

Sally Jo nodded and crawled across the hot cement toward her father. "Could I have some money, too?"

"Sure thing, kiddo." He slapped a crumpled bill into her hand. "Let me know if it won't take this, and I can quick run up." She hoped the machine didn't so she could follow him upstairs. She wondered if there was a bedroom for her, maybe it was painted canary yellow, like her one at home. Maybe he'd already started a bulletin board here, had set aside photographs of Bora Bora, the Sahara Desert, Antarctica.

Heading across the pool deck, a few steps behind Lucia, Sally Jo imagined what snacks they'd have. She'd once jotted down her top five vending machine picks: Reese's Pieces, Twinkies, Cheetos, Juicy Fruit Gum, and Peanut M&M's. She tried to arrange them in order, least to favorite, but couldn't. If they were out of Reese's Pieces, it was replaced with a Snickers. Plus, who knew when it was going to be a salty or a sweet day.

At the fitness center, covering most of the front door was a metal sign that read "No One Under 18 Allowed." Sally Jo slapped Lucia's arm. "We can't go in here."

"Hell if I care." Lucia yanked open the door. "After you."

Inside, through a small entryway, Sally Jo spotted a separate space for treadmills, another for dumb weights, and an empty studio with a ballet bar and wall-length mirrors. Between the men's and women's locker rooms were two vending machines.

"So, how long ago did your parents get divorced?" Lucia counted out her coins, made no eye contact.

"Well, my dad moved out a while ago, if that answers your question." It didn't feel right to tell Lucia the divorce hadn't yet been finalized.

"Oh." Lucia paced back and forth in front of the machines; it was obvious that she hadn't determined her own top five. On the wall near the towel desk, Sally Jo saw a photograph of a man who resembled her father. Same short brown hair, same mustache, same pearly whites. As she moved closer, she could make out the caption: "Most pull-ups in a minute." In front of the glossy print, without the glare from the overhead lights, she confirmed that it was indeed her father, his dark brown eyes peering back at her. Hers, too, since she'd inherited those eyes, or so everyone said. There were other photographs, all with captions: "Fastest 50-yard freestyle," "Longest long jump," and "Most lunges in a minute." Since her father had only lived at the complex for a short time, she was surprised to see that he was already competing in contests, had become so situated. Had made himself so at home.

From behind, Sally Jo could hear Lucia's stifled giggles. Sally Jo turned to see her clutching a bag of pretzels. Sally Jo wondered why anyone would choose something that you could get at home for free. "Is that your dad?" Lucia said, shielding her mouth as she chewed. In the picture, Sally Jo's father was flexing his muscles, without a smile, like a greased up bodybuilder.

"Oh, him? Guess so." Sally Jo flexed her own muscles, mocking him. She pointed outside. "Hey, Lucia, which way to the pool?"

Lucia copied her, though pointed to the weight machines. "Wait, first I need to do my leg presses." Sally Jo never knew Lucia was funny. She wondered what Lucia thought of their parents dating.

From behind the towel desk, Sally Jo nabbed a ballpoint pen. "Should I draw on him?" She took a step back to examine.

"You mean graffiti?" Lucia said. "Is anyone here?" Sally Jo scanned the fitness center, and other than a woman leisurely riding a stationary bike, the place was empty.

In an exaggerated, cartoonish way, Sally Jo tiptoed up to the photograph and scribbled a handlebar mustache onto the shiny picture. She added ticks of hair until the mustache was thick and unruly. After peering around to make sure no one had entered, she drew in bushy eyebrows and darkened one of his front teeth.

"There, that's better." It felt good to do something bad, since she'd always been good and where had that lead her? She stared at her handiwork, but must have paused too long because she felt Lucia jiggling her arm.

Sally Jo snapped back into focus when Lucia shoved her toward the exit. "It's time to go," Lucia said, "You rebel, you"

Sally Jo smiled. She'd never been referred to like that, never as a rebel.

As they made their way back to the pool deck, Sally Jo realized that her father and Rosalie weren't where they'd left them. Squinting against the bright sun, she spotted them in the hot tub seated next to another couple. All four of them were laughing. Sally Jo had never seen her father belly-laugh like that, at least not in response to anything she'd said. He was tossing back his head, clutching his stomach, and making a hissing sound that reminded her of air being let out of a tire.

"I think they're checking us out," Lucia said and cocked her head in the direction of two guys Sally Jo hadn't noticed. The boys were sitting on the edge of the pool and looked to be a few years older, most likely in high school.

"Let's walk by them," Lucia said.

"Forget the stupid chlorine. Let's swim." Sally Jo hoped the water would disguise her ugly stick legs.

"Whatever you say." Lucia shrugged her shoulders, dove in. When she resurfaced, her dark hair was slicked back, making her look even more beautiful, like a model in a Coppertone ad.

Sally Jo hoped not to get her hair wet, wanted to avoid turning into the wet gerbil she knew she'd resemble. After lowering herself to the pool's edge, she slid in. The water was warm, inviting. She doggy-paddled her way over to Lucia who was treading water a few feet from the edge where the boys were seated. Sally Jo had never seen anyone move so gracefully, so effortlessly; concurrent circles grew from Lucia as she sliced her legs through the water, and with her hands, she spread an invisible layer across the surface. Although, to Sally Jo's surprise, one of the boys—the one with darker hair wearing Bermuda shorts—seemed to be looking at her. Not at Lucia.

"What's your name?" he said. Sally Jo looked around and noticed Lucia had already swum across the pool and was now making her way up the ladder.

"Sally," she said to the boy. She'd never introduced herself like that, never without the "Jo."

"I'm Chris." He flashed her a smile, a wide one, the kind flaunted by boys who know they have perfect teeth and cute faces. "You live here?"

Sally Jo saw that Lucia and Chris' friend had now moved a few steps back from the water. The foil from a pack of cigarettes the boy was holding flickered in his palm. She wondered if Lucia smoked, too.

Sally Jo shifted her focus back to Chris, back to the tiny beads of sweat sprouting on his nose. Up close, she realized that he had the type of eyelashes her mother said were wasted on males.

"Nope, I don't live here. My dad does." She went to point out her father, but couldn't find him in the hot tub—she was sure the whirlpool was past capacity by now, but for some reason, she didn't seem to care. Sally Jo thought back to the days when her father never wanted her to date, said he would kill any guy who tried to make a pass at her, at his only daughter. She wondered if he would intervene now, especially since this guy, Chris, was clearly older.

"Earth to Sally." Chris waved his hand in front of her face.

"I'm sorry. It's just that chlorine makes my skin itch." She was beginning to wonder if she was one of those people who started to believe their own lies.

He invited her to sit with him, away from the water, at a table that had a pile of beach towels neatly folded on top.

"Is this your spot?" she asked. It didn't look like it had been saved by a kid.

"Sort of. My friend—Smooth Sam over there, the one hitting on your friend—well, his dad lives here. The guy gets up at 5:00 every morning to save himself a seat. Some days he never even comes down at all."

She knew Sam's dad was the kind of person her dad would've despised. Her mom, too. Hatred toward other people had always united them.

He reached his hand into a nylon backpack that had been stashed beneath the towels.

"Want some?" Sally Jo wondered if there was alcohol in there and if he was going to offer her a sip. Her first sip. When she saw him ripping open a pouch of sunflower seeds, she felt slightly disappointed.

On her way in, she'd remembered reading: "No seeds of any kind" posted along with the other pool rules. She considered telling him, but extended her hand instead.

"Sure." Chewing on seeds, spitting the salty shells into an empty 7-

up can, she found out that he lived here in Apple Valley and, in the fall, was going to be a sophomore at the high school. He asked her age.

"Freshman." Another lie, though he didn't seem to question it. Looking around, she noticed that Lucia and Smooth Sam had made their way out of the gated area and were now both leaning against the health club. Sally Jo figured they were seconds away from making out. Sally Jo had never kissed a boy. She suspected most of the girls in her grade had, and she knew Lucia had for sure. Sally Jo had heard that last winter, during a game of spin the bottle at a boy/girl party, several of the boys had intentionally stopped the bottle in front of Lucia. After two or three kisses, she apparently flipped them all off and left.

Sally Jo wasn't sure if Lucia's mom had noticed that her daughter had left the premises with a boy. Rosalie was still in the hot tub, and it didn't seem like she was paying attention.

Chris dug around in his backpack. "Hey, do you have any sunscreen I can borrow? I forgot mine."

She walked back to grab hers, past her dad who was busy entertaining a growing group of friends. Her mom used to hate it when her dad would hold court, especially for strangers. Sally Jo wished her mom were here to remind him to pay more attention to his daughter. Tell him to drop the stand-up comedy act, especially since Sally Jo had always been the one who laughed the hardest at his corny jokes.

Once Sally Jo returned, she handed the sunscreen to Chris. He rubbed some onto his chest and face, then dumped the rest of the container into his backpack. Sally Jo wanted to say something, but felt stupid. It was only sunscreen.

"Do you want to go see what our friends are up to?" Chris shot her a half smile—there were those straight white teeth again. She swept her tongue across her upper set of braces, hoped she didn't have any food stuck between the wires.

Sally Jo suspected Chris might want to kiss her, like their friends were doing. Kiss her, with braces on her teeth, kiss her even though she had skinny, white legs. Her first kiss. One of the many firsts she had to look forward to.

She peeked over at her father. She wondered if he was preparing to storm over, grab Chris by the collar, give him a piece of his mind. And if he wasn't, maybe it was because he hadn't noticed she'd been talking to a boy. "Hang on," she said and made her way over to the hot tub. She knelt down by her dad. Even though she hadn't seen any beer cans, she could smell the yeasty, stale stench on his breath and in the surrounding air, seeping from his pores.

"Dad? Did you see where Lucia went?" Anything to get him to look around.

"Nope, sorry Kiddo!" He said, without turning his head.

She was on her own. Her dad inched closer to a high-pitched blonde. Rosalie didn't seem to care, but Sally Jo's thoughts spun to her mother and how upset she used to get when her father paid more attention to other women.

"Only the pretty ones," her mother would say later on the phone to her sisters, Sally Jo's aunts.

Chris leaned against the exit sign, waiting for her. As they walked out, her eyes followed the backs of Lucia and Sam as they moved together, hand in hand, toward the parking lot. Chris guided her past the tennis courts, around a storage shed, and behind an evergreen tree. A blanket had been spread on the fallen pine needles. From there, all she could see was a slice of the parking lot and an empty laundry truck parked up against the gym.

"Is this okay?" Chris asked and lowered himself to the ground. She wasn't sure how to answer.

"So do you play any sports?" she asked, trying to make this—their location, what she was wearing, how they met—seem normal.

He leaned closer to her and kissed her neck. "Shhh," he whispered. Unsure of what to do, she hunched her shoulders.

"What's wrong?" he said.

"Nothing, it's just that my dad might walk by."

He sighed. "Hang on, I've got to take a whiz." He stood up and walked off. She glanced down at her legs, at the ugly scab and freckles, and knew she would never be the pretty one, the girl all the boys wanted to date. When he returned, she grabbed his face and kissed him, kissed him before he came to his senses and realized she was nothing special. His mouth tasted salty and his breath smelled of fish, not the first kiss she had imagined. Before she knew it, he had removed one swimsuit strap from her shoulder and was cupping her breast. First and second bases, two firsts. Gone and gone. She sat up tall, forcing his hand into an awkward position, stretched taller until he removed it.

"So how old is your friend? She's cute." Only the pretty ones. She now knew how her mother must have felt. She felt dumb, too, thinking Chris had been interested in her.

"Oh, Lucia?" she said. "Well, she's a huge slut. I don't know her well, but once during a game of spin the bottle, she gave out blow jobs instead of kisses." Sally Jo couldn't believe she had said that, especially since it wasn't true and Lucia didn't deserve it.

"Oh, well, she sounds like my kind of girl," Chris said and laughed. "Come here." He laid his hand on her inner thigh. Sally Jo didn't remove his hand, not right away. She had wasted two firsts on a boy she didn't even like. She thought of her mom and all the regrets her mother had claimed over the years. Maybe this was how it started: with one boy, one afternoon, and eventually your life becomes swept up by regret.

"I have to go," Sally Jo said, as she shot up. Moving in the direction of the pool, she considered turning around and telling Chris that her friend was not a slut, and how she'd made that story up. Tell him she regretted kissing him, had now wasted two firsts on a boy she never wanted to see again.

Instead, she made her way to the pool. She knew what she needed to do. She needed to call her mother and ask to be picked up early. But first she needed to tell her dad that although she appreciated the *National Geographic*s, she would only visit him here again if it were the two of them. Until then, Zimbabwe and Siberia—the world—would be on hold.

MATTHEW J SPIRENG
CHIPMUNK, MORNING RUN, BIG SKY, MONTANA

What did you see?
Oh, nothing.

Actually, beyond the trees—spruce
and lodgepole pine and aspen—and beyond
the wildflowers still thriving after frosts,

and fresh snow on the slopes only
a little higher up, Lone Mountain white
in the morning sun, beyond shadows on stumps

dark beneath the trees, and the meadows
of dried grasses, the huge old white pine still
hanging on near the road, beyond the sky

(cont)

clearing and a few clouds across the valley
at the height I was, beyond this, there was the chipmunk
eating on the edge of the road the exact same place

I saw it the day before, powder of whatever it gnawed
dusting the pavement at its chosen spot, and while yesterday
I was silent as I passed, today I said, "Hello."

Spireng

HARVESTING GINSENG WITH MY BROTHER (FOR RON)

This is anticipation,
for I do not know if my
50-acre woods offer anything
but promise, perhaps empty, for

I have never harvested ginseng before,
do not know if it grows here, as I
never knew of my brother before
last November, though I was 67,

adopted at birth. It is our first early fall
together and he is the ginseng expert,
so we will enter my woods looking
for what only he knows for certain.

I do not know what we will find, but
I will learn whether he first did this
as a child, alone or with other siblings
I did not know then either. I am his

older brother and had I been there
I might have taught him the harvest.
Instead, now it is I who will learn.
My brother will teach me what he knows.

Spireng

SPEAKING OF THE WEATHER IN UPSTATE NEW YORK, FEBRUARY

It remains to be seen if it will reach 70
in a few days, as they say it will, a record
if it does, but it snowed overnight and now

the ground is white except where the snow
has been disturbed. It's climbed to 40 at noon
and already the snow is melting. A stranger

this morning said how much he was looking forward
to 70, and I would be, too, if I didn't know
what such weather means. I'm childless, so maybe

I shouldn't be worried about life after I'm gone,
as seems the case for many with children, but, human
and childless, I know all in the future are mine.

Spireng

CONTRIBUTORS

JULIE OWSIK ACKERMAN's first novel, *Across the Border,* previously appeared in *Santa Fe Writers Project* (online). Her essays have appeared in *The Los Angeles Times, The Philadelphia Inquirer,* and *Bitch Magazine,* with one recent essay appearing in many outlets around the country including *The Chicago Tribune* and *msn.com*. Her experiences of living in Mexico and working as an immigration lawyer inspired this story. She teaches Girls Write Out, a writing workshop for women in Narberth, PA.

CHRISTOPHER AMENTA is a writer living in Boston, MA. He received his MFA from Boston University, where he was given the Saul Bellow Award and was named a Leslie Epstein Global Fellow. His writing has appeared in *Redivider, Boston College Magazine*, and *Holy Cross Magazine*. His first novel is currently on submission.

BETH BAYLEY is a writer, yoga instructor, and occasional archivist who divides her time between Massachusetts and Singapore. Her work has appeared or is forthcoming in *Ghost City Review, Neologism Poetry Journal, Slant, Vox Poetica*, and *Picaroon Poetry*, among others. Find her at bethbayley.yoga.

LAURA BERNSTEIN-MACHLAY's poetry and essays have appeared in *The American Scholar, Georgia Review, Into the Void, Michigan Quarterly Review, New Plains Review, Poetry Northwest, Redivider*, and many others. She currently has essays forthcoming in *Hotel Amerika, World Literature Today* and *The American Scholar*; She is the author of *Travelers*, a collection of creative-nonfiction essays. Her work has been nominated for multiple Pushcart Prizes in both the essay and poetry categories.

PAUL BOWMAN, former nursing home maintenance man, writes plays and fictions. His one-acts have been staged in theaters ranging from Long Island to San Diego and even across the waters in Australia. His stories, flash to full-length, have appeared in *The Chiron Review, Conceit, Downstate, The Listening Eye, Burnt Pine, Southern Fried Karma, Green Hills Literary Lantern*, and elsewhere.

PATRICIA CANTERBURY began her creative writing journey with a beginner's short-fiction class at a local community college. Since then, she has taken many courses, including, most recently, a poetry class. She has written several short-stories, four of which were published by *SandScript,* a national award-winning community college literary magazine. She is currently working on a novel and some short-fiction and nonfiction pieces.

NEIL CARPATHIOS is the author of five full-length poetry collections. His sixth, *The Door on Every Tear*, is slated to appear in 2020 from Wipf and Stock Publishers. He also edited the anthology, *Every River on Earth: Writing from Appalachian Ohio* (Ohio University Press, 2015). He is a professor of English and creative writing at Shawnee State University in Portsmouth, Ohio.

ROBERT CARR is the author of *Amaranth*, published in 2016 by Indolent Books, and *The Unbuttoned Eye*, a full-length 2019 collection from 3: A Taos Press. A poet and public health professional, he also serves as deputy director for The Bureau of Infectious Disease and Laboratory Sciences in Massachusetts. Among other publications, his poetry appears in *Crab Orchard Review*, *The Massachusetts Review*, *Rattle* and *Shenandoah*. He is development editor for poetry with Indolent Books, based in Brooklyn NY. Additional information can be found at robertcarr.org

MARISA P CLARK is a queer Southerner whose writing appears in *Apalachee Review*, *Cream City Review*, *Foglifter*, *Ontario Review*, *Pilgrimage*, and elsewhere, with work forthcoming in *Shenandoah*, *Dunes Review*, *Pangyrus*, and *Whale Road Review*, among others. She was twice the winner of the Agnes Scott College Writers' Festival Prizes (in fiction, 1996; in nonfiction, 1997), and in 2011 *Best American Essays* recognized her creative nonfiction among the Notable Essays. She lives in the Southwest.

MIKE COHEN is the author of *Rivertown Heroes* and *The Three of Us*. His short stories have appeared in *Streetlight, Adelaide, STORGY, Umbrella Factory, FRiGG Magazines* and *The American Writers* and *Penman Reviews*. His stories will appear/ have appeared in *The North Dakota Quarterly, Evening Street Review, and Litbreak Magazine.* A retired lawyer, he lives with his family in Seattle. *mikecohenauthor.com*; Facebook: Michael Cohen Author.

STEVE COUGHLIN is an associate professor of English at Chadron State College in northwest Nebraska. His collections of poetry include *Another City* (FutureCycle Press) and *Driving at Twilight* (Main Street Rag). He has published poems and essays in several literary journals, including the *Gettysburg Review*, *New Ohio Review*, *Michigan Quarterly Review*, *Rattle*, and *Slate.*

J. P. DALEY is retired and lovin' it. His career was spent in magazine publishing in New York City, working as a sales promotion copywriter for *The Reader's Digest*, *Redbook*, *McCall's*, *Times Mirro*r, and *Scholastic* magazines. Along the way, he completed studies for a bachelor's degree at Pace University. And is an active member of the Hudson Valley Writers' Workshop. Home is in the small village of Wappingers Falls, NY on the banks of the Hudson River.

STEVE DEUTSCH was born in Brooklyn, NY and lives in State College, PA. Over the last three years, his work has appeared in two dozen print and online journals. He was nominated for Pushcart Prizes in 2017 and 2018. His chapbook, *Perhaps You Can*, was published in 2019 by Kelsay Press.

NICKOLAS DUARTE is a writer and filmmaker. His scripted and documentary work has played in Academy Award qualifying festivals, has won an Emmy, been nominated for a Webby, received distribution through Sony Pictures Television, and featured on Short of the Week. He is a National Endowment of the Arts recipient and is currently developing a crime drama with Warner Bros. His poetry is inspired by the working class culture and Mexican mysticism of his childhood in Tucson, AZ.

LAUREN ELIZABETH is twenty-two years old and has been writing stories, both fiction and non-fiction, for over half that time. As a recent college graduate living in Boston, Massachusetts, Lauren spends her time drinking way too much iced coffee, working on her next literary piece, and doing her best to navigate adulthood. "Purple Dragonflies" is her first published work and a memoir of a childhood friend, who she still thinks of every day.

JONATHAN B FERRINI is a published author who resides in San Diego. He received his MFA in motion picture and television production from UCLA.

GARY GALSWORTH spent three years in the Marine Corps before studying painting and filmmaking at the Art Institute of Chicago and the University of Chicago. His work has been featured in *Abstract, Contemporary Expressions, Pennsylvania English, Broad River Review,*

Obsidian, Main Street Rag, and others. In addition to writing poetry, he is a professional plumber and a student of Zen and Vipassana practice. He's published three books of poems: *Yes Yes, Beyond the Wire,* and *Nothing Itself.* He lives in Hoboken, NJ.

MAUREEN GERAGHTY has taught high school for over 28 years, mostly in alternative school settings. She is the mother of two fantastic teenagers. Her poems, essays, and stories are published in *The National Writing Project, Re-Thinking Schools, Watch My Rising Anthology, Tacenda Literary Journal, Teaching with Heart, The Grief Dialogues,* mamazine.com, Mothering.com, *Look Up-Poems of a Life* and most recently a children's book, *Grandpa Ron's Bird Food.* She lives in Portland, Oregon.

PAULA GOLDMAN's book, *The Great Canopy,* won the Gival Press Poetry award. Her work has appeared in many magazines and anthologies. She holds an MA degree in Journalism from Marquette University and an MFA in Writing from Vermont College. Former reporter for *The Milwaukee Journal,* she served as a docent and lecturer at the Milwaukee Art Museum. A new book by Kelsay Books in Utah is forthcoming in 2020. She lives in Milwaukee, WI with her husband, Allan.

CHARLES HALSTED is a retired academic physician whose poetry education consists of ten successive on-line courses from Stanford Continuing Studies, several workshops, and participation in writers' retreats at Taos, Fishtrap, Squaw Valley, and Pebble Beach. His poems have been published in over thirty poetry journals, in a chapbook entitled *Breaking Eighty* and in a full-length book entitled *Extenuating Circumstances.*

WILLIAM HART is a fiction writer and poet whose work has appeared in several hundred literary journals, commercial magazines, newspapers and anthologies. He's published ten poetry collections, many short stories, and the novels *Never Fade Away (*Daniel and Daniel, 2002) and *Operation Supergoose (*Timberline Press, 2007). He also writes and helps produce documentaries for PBS with his filmmaker wife.

WILLIAM OGDEN HAYNES is a poet and author of short fiction from Alabama who was born in Michigan. He has published seven collections of poetry (*Points of Interest, Uncommon Pursuits, Remnants, Stories in Stained Glass, Carvings, Going South* and *Contemplations*) and one book of short stories *(Youthful Indiscretions)* all available on Amazon.com.

Over 175 of his poems and short stories have appeared in literary journals and his work is frequently anthologized. www.williamogdenhaynes.com

MARC KAMINSKY is the author of eight books of poems, including *A Cleft in the Rock* (Dos Madres Press), *The Road from Hiroshima* (Simon & Schuster) and *Daily Bread* (University of Illinois Press). His poems, fiction and essays have appeared in many magazines and anthologies, including *The Manhattan Review*, *The American Scholar*, *The Oxford Book of Aging*, and *Voices within the Ark: The Modern Jewish Poets*.

FRANCES KOZIAR is primarily a fiction writer of the contemporary fiction, high fantasy, and young adult genres, though she also publishes poetry and nonfiction. Her work has appeared in 25+ literary magazines, and she is seeking an agent for a diverse NA high fantasy novel. She is a young retired (disabled) academic and a social justice advocate. She lives in Kingston, Ontario, Canada.

TOM KROPP is a sensei in kenpo karate who has won numerous tournament awards. His Work has appeared in *Muscle and Fitness*, *Woodworker's Journal*, *Outdoor Life*, *Nut House*, *J Journal* and *Conceit* magazines.

GAIL LANGSTROTH is an international lecturer, eurythmy performer, and poet. She lives in Pittsburgh, PA, where she is an active member in the Mad Women in the Attic writing workshops. The Patricia Dobler Poetry Prize, 2011, Accents Chapbook Competition, finalist, 2014, and the Jeffster Award, 2014, account for some of her literary achievements. *Firegarden / jardín- de-fuego*, her duo-language manuscript, will be published by *Get Fresh Books,* 2020. www.wordmoves.com

VIVIAN LAWRY is Appalachian by birth, a psychologist by training, and a writer by passion. Her work has appeared in more than sixty literary journals and anthologies. In addition, she has published four books: *Dark Harbor*, *Tiger Heart*, *Different Drummer,* and *Nettie's Books*. Visit vivianlawry.com to read her blog, to see a complete list of publications, and to read samples of her work. She now lives and writes near Richmond, Virginia.

MARTIN H LEVINSON is a member of the Authors Guild, National Book Critics Circle, PEN America, and the book review editor for *ETC: A Review of General Semantics.* He has published nine books and numerous articles and poems. Website: martinlevinson.com

LISA LOW has a doctorate in English literature; she has taught at a variety of colleges and universities (Colby College, Waterville, Maine; University of Massachusetts, Amherst; Cornell College, Mt. Vernon, Iowa; Boston University; and Pace University, NYC). She has a scholarly book with Cambridge University Press; she was a theatre critic for Christian Science Monitor Broadcasting; and her poetry has appeared in *Aphros*, *Anteaus*, *Phoebe*, *Intro 11*, *Potomac Review*, *Delmarva Review*, and *Crack the Spine*.

CLARE COOPER MARCUS is professor emerita of architecture and landscape architecture at UC Berkeley. The author of six professional books and a personal memoir, she began writing poetry 6 years ago as a member of the Deep River group at the C G Jung Institute of San Francisco.

KATHLEEN MCGOOKEY's fourth book, *Instructions for My Imposter,* is available from Press 53. Her latest chapbook *Nineteen Letters* was published by BatCat Press. Her work has appeared in *Copper Nickel*, *Crazyhorse*, *December*, *Field*, *Glassworks, Miramar*, *Ploughshares*, *Prairie Schooner*, *Quiddity*, and *Sweet*. She has received grants from the French Ministry of Foreign Affairs and the Sustainable Arts Foundation. She lives in Middleville, MI with her family.

LISA MECKEL's poetry has been published in *Rattle*, *Nimrod International Journal*, *Reed Magazine*, *The MacGuffin*, *Mirboo North Times*, *Australia*, *Euphony Journal*, *Pennsylvania English*, and many others. She is a three-time winner of the Poetry Prize at the Santa Barbara Writers Conference and was a presenter for The Big Read, honoring poet Robinson Jeffers. She is currently assembling a collection of her poems for publication.

ANITA PINATTI lives in a quiet corner of New England where she enjoys the challenge of combining her poetry and photography. She has done exhibits in libraries throughout New England and received a Juror's Choice award in a Flash Ekphrastic poetry event at the Hartford Art School, University of Hartford (Connecticut). Her poems have appeared in *Common Ground Review*, *Ekphrasis*, and *Vallum*.

ANTHONY RABY is a poet and writer, who published his first collection of fiction and poetry, *Fractured Minds and Lost Souls,* in 2018. He is currently pursuing a bachelor's degree through Adams State University's Correspondence Program. When not viciously attacking a typewriter, he is usually doing some other creative activity or reading.

FAYE REDDECLIFF was born and grew up in central Pennsylvania. After graduating from the University of Pittsburgh, she moved to Chicago for a while and then moved on to northern California where she now lives and enjoys daily walks with her two dogs. She writes both fiction and non-fiction and has had her work published in various magazines.

DOLLY REYNOLDS' prose has appeared in numerous literary journals including *Euphony, Cheat River Review, North American Review, Lullwater Review, Phoebe, Worcester Review, Red Wheelbarrow, Portland Review, decomP,* and *Gemini Magazine.* She has been twice nominated for a Pushcart Prize, and holds an MFA from San Francisco State, where she received the Wilner Award for short fiction. She grew up in New England, and lives in San Francisco with her family.

BARBARA SABOL is the author of the poetry collection, *Solitary Spin,* and two chapbooks, *Original Ruse* and *The Distance Between Blues.* Her awards include an Individual Excellence Award from the Ohio Arts Council and the Mary Jean Irion Poetry Prize. She reviews poetry books for the blog, *Poetry Matters.* She is a speech therapist who lives in Akron, OH.

MICHAEL SANDLER began to publish about ten years ago, having written for the desk drawer for much of his adulthood. His poems have since appeared in 35+ journals including *Crack The Spine, Valparaiso Poetry Review,* and *Zone 3.* His first collection of poems, *The Lamps of History,* is forthcoming from FutureCycle Press. His author website is sandlerpoetry.com.

ROCHELLE JEWEL SHAPIRO has published essays in the *NYT* (Lives), *Newsweek, Empty Mirror,* and many anthologies. Her poetry has appeared in such publications as the *Iowa Review, Moment, Reunion: The Dallas Review, Compass Rose, Steam Ticket, Slipstream, Moment,* and more. She currently teaches writing at UCLA extension. rochellejshapiro.com

MICHAEL J SHEPLEY is a writer living and working in Sacramento. In the realm of short fiction his stories have appeared in, or/&, @ *Verdad, Snail Mail Revue, AtlanticPacific Review, MAP & London Magazine.*

MATTHEW J SPIRENG's book *What Focus Is* was published by WordTech Communications. His book *Out of Body* won the 2004 Bluestem Poetry Award and was published by Bluestem Press. He won *The MacGuffin*'s 23rd Annual Poet Hunt in 2018 and is a 10-time Pushcart Prize nominee. His latest book, *Good Work* (Evening Street Press, 2020), won the 2019 Sinclair Poetry Prize.

VINCENT J TOMEO is a poet, archivist, historian, and community activist. He is published in *The New York Times*, *Comstock Review*, *Mid-America Poetry Review*, *EDGZ*, *Spires*, *Tiger's Eye*, *By Line*, *Mudfish*, *The Blind Man's Rainbow*, *The Neo Victorian/Cochlea*, *The Latin Staff Review*, and *Grandmother Earth* (VII THRU XI), etc. To date, he has 899 published poems/essays, winner of 105 awards, 133 public readings.

MEREDITH TREDE's books are *Tenement Threnody, Field Theory,* and a chapbook, *Out of the Book.* Other extensive journal publications include *Barrow Street, Friends Journal, Gargoyle,* and *Paris Review.* Meredith was granted Blue Mountain Center, Ragdale, Saltonstall and VCCA fellowships, and the Nicholson Political Poetry Award. She holds a Sarah Lawrence College MFA, a New School MA, a BA from SUNY, Oneonta, and serves on the Slapering Hol Press Advisory Committee. www.meredithtrede.com.

SUSAN TRIEMERT holds an MA in Education and is soon to complete her MFA from Hamline University in St. Paul, MN. She has been published in *Colorado Review, Cheat River Review, Crab Orchard Review, A-Minor* and elsewhere. She lives in St. Paul with her husband, their two sons, and way too many animals.

DENNIS VANNATTA is a Pushcart and Porter Prize winner, with stories published in many magazines and anthologies, including *River Styx, Chariton Review, Boulevard,* and *Antioch Review*. His sixth collection of stories, *The Only World You Get,* was recently published by Et Alia Press.

ANNETTE VELASQUEZ is the proud daughter of Hungarian refugees and for over three decades poetry has been her passion. Currently she resides in El Paso, Texas where she advocates for the rights of immigrants/refugees and the disabled. She is also active in the local literary scene, including the Tumblewords Project and Papagayo Project. She lives with her hubby and 2 rambunctious cats.

TONY VICK, currently incarcerated in a Tennessee prison for 24 years, is author of *Secrets from a Prison Cell, (A Convict's Eyewitness Accounts of the Dehumanizing Drama of Life Behind Bars)*, Cascade Books 2018. Raised in a conservative Christian home, he held the fact that he was gay for 34 years and is now active in prison reform and bringing awareness about human rights issues.

THOMAS A WEST, JR has had over 200 poems published in little and literary magazines, including *The Ann Arbor Review, The Aurorean, California Quarterly, The Connecticut River Review, The Listening Eye, The Literary Review, New Mexico Humanities Review, The New Renaissance, POEM, The Tampa Review, Wisconsin Review*, etc. He is author of *The Hungry Man* chapbook, published by Orchard Street Press, and *Nonantum Street*, a volume of poetry. He passed away in September 2019.

JENNIE WHITE is an emerging writer from Moline, IL, having recently graduated from Bradley University where she studied creative writing, sociology, and marketing. During her time at Bradley, she served as an editor of the creative arts magazine, *Broadside: Writers and Artists*, and on the executive board of Writehouse Ink. Much of her work confronts the effects of barring discussion of taboo subjects both in society and families.

MADELINE WISE grew up in Washington State and is a graduate of the University of Washington. She lives with her husband in Saint Helena, California. She is a member of Solstice Writers and Napa Valley Writers. Her short fiction has appeared in *American Fiction Volume 13, Bryant Literary Review, Front Range Review, North Atlantic Review, Palo Alto Review,* and other literary magazines.

LIZA WOLFF-FRANCIS is a literary artist with an MFA in Creative Writing from Goddard College. Her writing has appeared in *Steam Ticket, eMerge, Minute Magazine, Poetry Pacific, Edge*, and on various blogs. She has a poetry chapbook out called *Language of Crossing* (2015, Swimming with Elephant Publications), and she loves breakfast food.